DATE DUE

Racing With Catastrophe:
Rescuing America's Higher Education

Freedom House

Freedom House is an independent nonprofit organization that monitors human rights and political freedom around the world. Established in 1941, Freedom House believes that effective advocacy of civil rights at home and human rights abroad must be grounded in fundamental democratic values and principles.

In international affairs, Freedom House continues to focus attention on human rights violations by oppressive regimes, both of the left and the right. At home, we stress the need to guarantee all citizens not only equal rights under law, but equal opportunity for social and economic advancement.

Freedom House programs and activities include bimonthly and annual publications, conferences and lecture series, public advocacy, ongoing research of political and civil liberties around the globe, and selected, on-site monitoring to encourage fair elections.

Focus on Issues
General Editor: James Finn

This publication is one in a series of Focus on Issues. The separate publications in this series differ in the method of examination and breadth of the study, but each focuses on a single, significant political issue of our time. The series represents one aspect of the extensive program of Freedom House. The views expressed are those of the authors and not necessarily those of the Board of Freedom House.

About the Author

Richard Gambino is professor of educational philosophy at Queens College, City University of New York, and a member of the board of Freedom House. He has written extensively on issues concerning higher education.

Racing With Catastrophe:
Rescuing America's Higher Education

Richard Gambino

Focus on Issues, No. 13

Freedom House

First published in 1990.

Cover design by Emerson Wajdowicz Studios, N.Y.C

Distributed by arrangement with:
University Press of America, Inc.
4720 Boston Way
Lanham, MD 20706

3 Henrietta Street
London WC2E 8LU England

Library of Congress Cataloging-in-Publication Data

Gambino, Richard
     Racing with catastrophe : rescuing America's higher education /
    Richard Gambino
          p.   cm. — (Focus on issues : no. 13)
    Includes index.
    ISBN 0-932088-49-X. — ISBN 0-932088-50-3 (pbk.)
     1. Education, Higher—United States. 2. Education, Higher United
States—Aims and objectives. 3. Universities and colleges—United
States—Administration. 4. Educational innovations—United States.
1. Title. II. Series: Focus on issues (Freedom House (U.S.)) : 13.
LA227.3.036   1990
378.73—dc20   90-39353
                                            CIP

Dedication

In faith to all those of independent
mind who gladly learn and who gladly teach

Acknowledgement

I want to thank James Finn and Irwin H. Polishook for their help in the preparation of this book through their advice, comments, suggestions and corrections. Responsibility for the contents of the book and for the opinions expressed in it is, of course, solely mine.

Richard Gambino
New York
1990

Contents

Overview   1

Reforms Old and New   15

The Paideia of American Higher Education   39

Liberal Education: Purposes and Curricula   59

Governance and Constituents   79

The Open Society, Social Justice, and Power   95

Finances: Facts, Fictions and Fancies   109

"Human history becomes more and more a race between education and catastrophe."
—H.G. Wells, 1920

1.

Overview

THE AUTHORITY of learning and of the learned. Today the concept strikes many Americans, even within the faculties of colleges and universities, as an atavism, a somewhat stuffy and embarrassing throwback to more simple times. The concept is usually ignored in many discussions today regarding higher education. When it is approached, as it inevitably must be whenever basic questions about higher education are probed beyond surface levels, people usually back away from it. They retreat to the conceptually easier, practical problems suffered by colleges and universities, however difficult these are. These practical problems are so numerous that, desiring to or not, it is easy to spend all of one's energies at this level. In addition, the uneasiness felt about higher education's loss of essence makes many more than willing to remain on the practical surface level.

Further, it is easy to stay with relative superficialities because the size, scope and complexity of higher education are as intimidating as they are beguiling.

But any question about the reform of education must come down to the purposes of education in a democratic society. It must be remembered that this core concern lies below the turbulent surface, even as we survey the immediate problems.

Higher education is a major industry. Its annual operating outlay is about $125 billion, about equal to that of the communications industry and more than either the agriculture or automotive industries. In 1988, almost 7 million students were enrolled full-time in American colleges and universities, and another 5.4 million were enrolled and working part-time toward degrees. They paid as much as $19,000 per year for the privilege. An additional 20 million people took nondegree courses or programs of study.

Higher education employs two million people. In addition to its massive teaching mission, it produces about half of all research conducted in the United States. And recent major changes in higher education took place rapidly. Higher education's bigness is as new as, for example, that of the hi-tech communications industry. Enrollments in two-year colleges today alone exceed the total enrollments of thirty years ago.

Moreover, higher education is a major determinant of American culture and society, and has for a long time been popularly regarded as such. This is so much so that Daniel J. Boorstin in *The American Experience*, published in 1973, speaks of the "American religion of education."

Yet an uncomfortable realization that higher education is also in great crisis keeps presenting itself. It is widely being criticized as poorly serving students, who pay up to $80,000 for a bachelor's degree, and poorly serving the nation, endangering the future of both individuals and country. Boorstin says colleges, once "places of worship," have lost their purpose, and denigrates them as "hotels of the mind."

Robert Nisbet, in *The Idea of Progress*, published in 1980, says that the American faith in education revolved around historic faith in progress. With the loss of the crucial premises of the mystique of progress—belief in the value of the past, the worth of Western culture, faith in reason, science and technology, a sense of the sacred in life, faith in American institutions—and skepticism or fear about the consequences of personal and social "growth," the *mysterium tremendum* of Boorstin's education as a religion is gone. In the most profound, albeit ill-conceived, critique to date, Allan Bloom says American colleges and universities represent *The Closing of the American Mind*, meaning a descent into intellectual and moral nihilism.

Other scholars, such as Diane Ravitch, have elaborated on the institutional characteristics marking the problems of higher education: faculty demoralization and faculty unionization, open enrollment, student power and control, the sprawl of the "multiversity," increased access to higher education, affirmative action, increased federal regulation and mushrooming costs.

2

A more simple approach is taken in another genre of books. In the words of a favorable *New York Times* reviewer of one of them, they are in the vein of H.L. Mencken's panacea for reforming higher education: "Burn the buildings and hang the professors." One of the more recent of these books is journalist Charles J. Sykes' 1989 work *Professors and the Demise of Higher Education.*

Among Sykes' recommendations is the abolition of tenure. This would have a remarkably depressing effect on academic freedom, not to mention its implicit encouragement to colleges to continue their cost-saving exploitation of grossly underpaid part-time faculty. As we will see, part-timers currently teach 41 percent of all undergraduate college classes. Another of Sykes' suggestions is to relieve college teachers of the requirement that they publish. The effect of this, too, on the quality of instructors should not be hard to imagine. As we will see, the splitting of faculty into "teachers" and "researchers" would have unhealthy effects on education. Sykes shows little understanding of the value of classroom teachers being personally involved in scholarship and research. Indeed, he seems to regard study, scholarship and research as irresponsible evasions of teaching.

Sykes' suggestions are part of a larger expedient being widely advocated. It involves a whole-hearted embrace of the dualism of teaching versus research. These questions require much more critical examination than they have so far received.

John Rawls' statement of an ideal of equality of *result,* as well as of opportunity, in *A Theory of Justice* provided, unwittingly, a justification for many of the liberal and leftist campus reforms of the 1960s, 1970s and into the 1980s. It isn't that Rawls motivated the movement that radically altered much in American higher education. Rather, his theory gives the most coherent expression of a rationale for forces that rocked the campuses and fundamentally changed them in the 60s and 70s. Rawls' book has been enormously influential—a mere bibliography of commentaries on it ran to over 800 pages by 1982. A critique of Rawls' theory, especially as it pertains to higher education, is essential.

From another side, the 1980s saw the increasing commercialization of education in many ways. One of them resulted from a 1980 change in the copyright law. It grants universities automatic ownership of patents arising from federally funded research, and the right to license the patents to private corporations. This, joined with schools' increasing

3

need for research funds from corporations, interlocking directorates made up of executives from private corporations, foundations and university trustees and presidents, and the great influence of "blue ribbon" commissions made up from this interlocking network, all push higher education to meet the personnel, technological and research and development needs of corporate America at the expense of balanced, comprehensive, liberal education.

Because most grants from corporations are *not* designated for the general operations budgets of the universities, David F. Noble, of the National Coalition of Universities in the Public Interest, charges that universities "are looting their assets to support their commercial ventures, which promise little educational reform." All of this aggravates a major financial crisis in higher education, a crisis in which faculty pay lags behind the ever-rising cost of living, while tuitions rise sharply ever upward. (Tuition accounts, on average, for over 50 percent of higher education's annual revenues, and in the case of many schools much more than 50 percent.)

A spate of negative evaluations of elementary and high schools in the early 1980s culminated in the 1983 report, *A Nation at Risk*. These evaluations led to a national effort to improve schools at those levels. More recently, the spotlight has shifted to higher education. As noted, several high-powered commissions, committees, panels and forums have issued reports. Their criticisms have been severe, and such negative findings are likely to grow in number and bite during the next years. For example, several lengthy reports on higher education have been published in the last years, sponsored by the United States government and by major foundations.

Moreover, the very issuance of these reports is almost as significant as their content. Historically, reports by prestigious commissions and committees are the levers used by powerful groups to accomplish major changes in higher education. That is exactly what is happening today. Follow-up surveys show that the reports have had great influence. In addition, the reports have been followed by forums, e.g., the ongoing ones held by the powerful Business-Higher Education Forum, and articles in the professional and popular press, bringing irresistible pressures to bear on colleges.

The reports, forums, books and articles have some criticisms in common, but vary greatly in others, and also in many recommendations. In

4

many cases, their criticisms and recommendations are contradictory—as is typical of national opinion at large.

In sum, the future of higher education is up for grabs, and not only individuals but powerful lobbies are already contesting with each other to decide what that future will be.

Higher education in the U.S. today is ripe for obvious criticism and reform. It is lacking in purpose and coherence, and is "servile" rather than "liberal," meaning it has been subordinated to ends other than educational ones. And it is very expensive.

Reforms in education historically have been characterized by extreme swings. As John Dewey noted as early as 1904:

...the tendency of educational development [is] to proceed by reaction from one thing to another, to adopt for one year, or for a term of seven years, this or that new study or method of teaching, and then abruptly to swing over to some new educational gospel.

Until the late 1960s, American colleges were characterized by firm academic authority, expressed, for example, in a high degree of standardization in curricular content, modes of teaching (the traditional lecture approach), and in testing and grading. Academic requirements were highly structured, and sometimes rigid, as in "lock-step" programs of required courses often adding up to 50 percent or more of each student's total course credits during a college career. Courses and programs of study were made up almost exclusively of traditional subject matter interpreted in traditional ways. And in the *in loco parentis* doctrine, colleges exercised considerable control over the personal life of students.

In the turmoil of the Vietnam War period, the pendulum swung the other way, to an extreme. Colleges abdicated virtually all of their *in loco parentis* authority. Also, moves were made toward interdisciplinary studies, ethnic studies, women's studies, less formal or rigorous classroom instruction and work-study approaches—each with uneven success. Those students and programs adhering to the highest scholarly standards of the humanities and social sciences contributed to knowledge and understanding. Those studies and programs claiming special illumination through nonuniversal methods and standards often cause great heat, but shed little light.

But colleges also gave away much of their academic authority, in what a 1984 National Endowment for the Humanities report calls "a collective failure of nerve and faith on the part of both faculty and academic administrators." In the face of vocal, often raucous, vile or violent agitation by some students, some faculty and others for "relevant" studies, studies that purportedly would serve the reform and even the "revolution" of society, required courses were largely dropped. More important, the power to determine curricular matters and university governance was shared with students, and in many ways was, in effect, turned over to them.

The prevailing mood was egalitarian and anti-intellectual, characterized by slogans like "Don't trust anyone over thirty," and "Power to the people." Studies by major foundations and prominent academic figures joined the often mindless assault on the authority of the learned and of learning, making no distinction between that authority and the raw authoritarianism of naked political power. Authority was equated with authoritarianism to be struck down. As one example of many, in the 1971 book *How To Change Colleges,* Harold Taylor, the late president of Sarah Lawrence College, excoriated faculty for defending traditional educational values and explicitly called for turning curricular matters and governance over to students. In his influential book, Taylor wrote:

> I argue that in order to reach the problem of violence on campuses, we must start a great deal farther back, and not only put students on boards of regents and boards of trustees, but give them full responsibility for self-government on the campus and a position of equality with the administrative officers with whom they deal. The same kind of relationship should exist in the educational policy-making with the faculty.

Many faculty, representing authentic traditions, resisted ill-considered changes. But other faculty were in the forefront of those who undermined the authority of learning and the learned. Some actually believed the egalitarian anti-"elite," anti-intellectual cant of the time. Others thought even modest changes required major upheavals. Still others were politically hostile to "establishment" authorities and used colleges as targets of opportunity in their fight. Many, probably most, just acquiesced.

The result was undergraduate education in the 1980s that was skewed, subordinated to non-educational ends and, in intrinsically educational terms, mostly purposeless and meaningless. Damning statistics abound. Seventy-five percent of those graduates awarded baccalaureate degrees in 1983 had taken no course in European history; 72 percent, no course in American history; 86 percent, no course in classical Greek or Roman civilizations. Fewer than 50 percent of U.S. colleges require any foreign language study, down from 90 percent in 1966, and study of foreign languages has dropped to a low point. Since 1970, the number of majors in modern languages has declined by 50 percent, in philosophy by 62 percent, and in English by 57 percent. Since 1977, the number of freshmen intending to major in the physical sciences declined by 13 percent, in the humanities by 17 percent, in the social sciences by 19 percent, and in the biological sciences by 21 percent.

Between 1977 and 1982, the proportion of bachelor's degrees given in the arts and sciences, as opposed to vocational and professional degrees, dropped from 49 percent to 36 percent. Indeed, if the undergraduates of the 1980s are any indication, the American population of the future will be one made up largely of narrowly educated accountants doing the books of narrowly educated computer specialists and lawyers. "Less lucrative" and not so trendy vocations, among them college teaching, will be greatly understaffed.

To blame students and their families for this educational short-sightedness is, in my opinion, scapegoating. The responsibility lies with the colleges, which do not provide educational leadership or authority, and have allowed themselves to become "self-service cafeterias." This legacy of the Vietnam War period was aggravated in the 1980s by the practice of many financially pressed colleges of chasing after potential students by pandering to their most ignorant, callow and short-sighted careerist perceptions of their needs, while ignoring the needs of the nation, the most essential of these being the needs of a democratic society.

The egalitarian mood of the Vietnam period, and the pressure at that time to keep young men in college and therefore out of the military draft, contributed to a lowering of standards and to grade inflation. Today, it is widely believed that the inflation is at least a full point over twenty-five or thirty years ago. For example, a grade of "A" today is worth no more than, and perhaps less than, a "B" in the early 1960s. A 1980 study of 180 colleges done for the Evaluation Service at the Michigan State University found that the inflation of grades had stopped, but had not been reversed. The level of grades stabilized at standards inflated beyond those prevalent before 1960. There is no indication that the inflation has been reversed since 1980. Yet some small signs of tightening standards was

7

evident in the 1980 study. For example, some colleges were again count-
ing grades of "F" in students' grade point averages, a practice they had
dropped during the late 1960s and early 1970s.

The belief that standards have plummeted is supported by the fact that
there was a decline from 1964 to 1982 in eleven of fifteen disciplines
in which Graduate Record Exams are offered. The "GREs" are nationally
administered exams taken by college seniors, presumably among the brightest who want to go on to graduate or professional schools.

In 1985, a study of *graduates* of four-year colleges reported by the
National Center for Educational Statistics found that five out of ten whites
and eight out of ten blacks could not pass a "basic literacy" test. The
test consisted of such problems as reading and restating a long newspaper
column, reading a bus schedule, and calculating the tip from a restaurant
bill.

Although this book addresses mostly four-year undergraduate colleges,
many of their predicaments are common to two-year community colleges and to graduate schools as well. For example, the crises of standards
and purpose permeate the community colleges, and are spreading to the
graduate schools, even to the level of doctoral education. In its 29 March
1989 issue, *The Chronicle of Higher Education* reported that some departments in some graduate schools have done away with the requirement that
a student write, and be examined on, a dissertation for the PhD degree,
and that many more schools are considering following the precedent. The
reason given by those who advocate the change is that the dissertation
requirement is too hard on students; it places too great a burden on them.
This sentiment is based on a study by the National Research Council which
found that it now takes 6.9 years on average for a student to earn a doctoral degree, compared with 6.1 years in 1977.

Thus the Council of Graduate Schools and the Association of Graduate Schools have set up committees to take on this "problem." Proposals
are being advanced that PhD students be allowed to substitute a collection
of unrelated articles they've written, or to which they have contributed
in lieu of a dissertation. Indeed this practice is already in place in some
departments at some graduate schools, for example, at Cornell University.

Also, it is being proposed that several students be allowed to submit
the same "jointly authored" article in lieu of a dissertation, and that *each*
student get credit as the *sole* author, an approach said to be already surrepti-

tiously practiced at the University of Chicago and other schools. In fact, this practice is defended, and recommended to other schools, by the Dean of Physical Sciences at the University of Chicago, Stuart A. Rice. In his defense of this practice, Dean Rice was quoted by *The Chronicle of Higher Education* as making astonishing assertions:

> What determines acceptability is the quality of the work. That is not an issue which is determined by the number of authors.
>
> The rules are flexible enough that if you get special offprints [of articles] made with the other names [of authors] taken off, that is acceptable. That may seem like fraud, but it is acceptable.

Dean Rice went further, saying that in actual practice at the University of Chicago's Graduate School, the university's "nitpicking rules," as he termed them, prohibiting the practice of jointly authored articles are surreptitiously evaded by some departments which allow jointly written articles to be submitted under one name alone as satisfying the requirement in lieu of a dissertation for the PhD degree. "So," Dean Rice says, "if the rules say it must be a single-author article, they'll [the graduate departments] find a way to make it a single-author article."

In short, the reforms of the 60s and 70s were carried to extremes. My purpose is not recrimination, but 1) to stop their continuing excesses into the 1990s, and 2) to reverse another set of extreme, servile, short-sighted reforms initiated in the late 1980s that swing in different directions.

Curricular reform demands particular attention, stressing that each college must determine what every educated person "needs to know," provided that there be no return to the worst pedantic, formalistic requirements approach of the 1950s with its emphasis on mere accumulation of facts, to the neglect of deeper understanding. We must recognize that there will be substantial differences between colleges on this question. Such diversity reflects and furthers the richness of the American mind and culture. Both mind and culture suffer today from increasing homogenization in the U.S.—partly a result of the power of pop culture—making diversity in higher education more needed than ever. There is room for different approaches to the mastering of the basic models of thought employed in the humanities, the social sciences and the natural sciences. Education will benefit from evaluating these different approaches.

Most important, then, are two questions. First, what does it mean to educate a student in the late twentieth century? Second, what are the proper ends and means of higher education in a democratic society? The answers to both questions hinge on the central thesis of this book, that there is a legitimate, describable and defensible authority of learning, and that authority should place the learned and the institutions of learning in unique categories of responsibilities and privileges in a free, open and democratic society.

From this perspective, the questions of what roles different college constituencies—administrators, faculty, trustees, students, business, government, etc.—*should* have in determining curricula, in governance, and other critical educational issues, and what roles they *in fact* have today, are of major importance. Critical attention needs to be given to those views which advocate making education subservient to national interest goals, e.g., the United States' international economic competitiveness, and domestic political, social, moral and religious reforms.

The great majority of Americans, even those with good college educations, know very little about how colleges function. Lack of this knowledge restricts the ability of students, parents, alumni, supporters, citizens and taxpayers to think constructively about colleges. Just as war is too important to leave entirely to generals, higher-education is too important to remain a mysterious "guild" understood only by the initiated. The governance of colleges and universities, I argue, is inseparable from the major philosophical questions of purpose regarding higher education.

An institutional model of colleges needs to be offered, along with an interpretation of why collegial institutions evolved as they did. Both the ideal and actual functions and powers of the constituent groups—trustees, administrators, faculty, students and alumni associations—need examination. We need also to look closely at the different ways in which outsiders, e.g., foundations, business groups, political factions and government, sometimes seek to short-circuit the collegial system, and to examine what happens when they succeed in by-passing it. As examples, we have the politically motivated reforms of the 1960s and 1970s, as well as the attempts from very different, business-oriented directions made in the 1980s.

It is necessary to evaluate the elaborate, complicated, intense and not infrequently fierce, "medieval" ways in which power is shared and decisions are negotiated and made between trustees, administrators, faculty, students, etc., and the resulting "Byzantine" nature of campus politics. The traditional power-sharing collegial constitution of colleges explains to some extent why administrators and faculty have had tense relations, and also why intra- and inter-departmental politics are as strained as they are. But in the last twenty-five years, a major change has occurred in these tensions, reflecting the colleges' stances vis-á-vis other institutions—political, governmental and economic. In the past, administrations and faculties differed over how each should serve a common set of goals; today there is an unhealthy divergence over the goals and the priorities of those goals.

There are important committees on campuses, about which the typical student or graduate knows next to nothing, e.g., the departmental personnel and budget committees ("P&Bs"). These are most critical regarding the nature and quality of a college, both in the short-term and long-term. Today, committees are made up increasingly of faculty who were students during the Vietnam era, on the one hand, and a decreasing number of older faculty who received their graduate education and the academic ethos that went with it prior to the mid-1960s, on the other hand. The internal conflicts of perceptions and biases of many of the P&Bs present problems in reforming colleges.

An old jibe has it that academic politics is so fierce because so little is at stake. This is at once both true and false. The minutest details of issues are often disputed, so the process frequently appears at any given moment as petty. But from the nature of shared collegial power, big issues usually get settled by picking over every small item. From this reality flows the organization and structure, in a word, the "constitution" of colleges.

Examination of higher education's constitution must include the change in the roles of college presidents, from pre-World War II "chief educator among equals," to post-war managers, to today's fundraisers, public relations socializers, who have to give absurd amounts of time to all sorts of things other than education. The *de facto* priorities placed on presidents' time and energies need to be changed. Most important, it is necessary to reverse the 1980s' push toward making presidents analogous to corporate CEOs, which is at the heart of another effort to bypass faculty in academic reform, as was done in the 1960s and 1970s.

Faculty today are demoralized—by loss of real earning power, by academic authority lost (and, in part, given away) in the 1960s and 1970s, by attempts to further reduce their authority in the 1980s and to solve the problems of the colleges at their expense, e.g., by increasing their teaching loads and holding down their salaries. They are disheartened by the massive use of exploited part-time instructors, and by proposals to turn most faculty into nonresearch "classroom specialists," i.e., *de facto* high school teachers. The role of the faculty is absolutely critical to the future of higher education, and needs fresh examination, without whitewashing.

More than two-fifths of college students today hold jobs (and the figure is rising). The percentage of nontraditional students (i.e, those other than the seventeen to twenty-two year old, single person, dependent on parents) is rising. By 1992 *half* of all students will be older than twenty-five, and 20 percent will be over thirty-five. These facts require an exploration of the purposes of higher education beyond the traditional "college years" of ages seventeen to twenty-two.

Critical questions of financing colleges and of financing college education need rethinking, first by exploding some myths, e.g, the distinction between private and public institutions, a distinction which has become more and more a metaphor, then by making specific recommendations. Citing financial crises, even some of the wealthiest, best-endowed schools in the United States are cutting back academic programs, almost invariably in the humanities and social sciences.

Among the studies and programs to be eliminated, by gradual steps, is the entire sociology department at Washington University in St. Louis, a department reputed to be one of the best in the nation. Columbia University is phasing out entirely both its geography and linguistics departments. And Johns Hopkins University over a period of five years will eliminate several arts and sciences departments. Areas in the humanities and social sciences are often termed "exotic" by college administrators and trustees.

They certainly are exotic—in one regard. They do not attract the off-campus financial grants to colleges that the physical sciences attract, making these latter departments more independent of the college's budget, and hence more immune from cutbacks. The point is not to open a competition between areas of study. On the contrary, it is to point out that college administrations and trustees set up such conflicts, and that they then resolve the conflicts on their *own*. In other words, in the guise of "necessary cost-cutting," administrations and trustees of colleges are making vital academic decisions, both in this context and in others as well. The decisions they are making are devastating to higher education. The financial supporters and financial administrators of higher education, I will show, are using their leverage to become the masters of the purpose, content and future of higher education. Running through the 1980s, their efforts have led to the ever increasing commercialization of higher education. The views and interests of the commercial sectors of American society are increasingly determining how a college's resources are set and allocated.

2.

Reforms Old and New

IN APRIL of 1987, a jury in Massachusetts brought in a verdict in a trial of fifteen defendants charged with trespassing and disorderly conduct. The case brought a sense of *deja vu* to anyone who witnessed the disruptions of American campuses by the New Left, its allies, and its coactivists in the Vietnam period. One of the defendants in the trial was Amy Carter, the nineteen-year-old daughter of former President Jimmy Carter.

Amy Carter and the other defendants had disrupted an effort by CIA recruiters at the University of Massachusetts at Amherst in November of 1986. Their legal defense was ingenious, not to say disingenuous. They invoked an old common law, commonsense precept that the breaking of a law is justified if the lawbreaker was acting to prevent a "clear and imminent danger." For example, one is justified in the normally illegal act of breaking into a house if the house is on fire and the purpose of the break-in is to rescue the house's occupants.

The "danger" cited by the defendants in the Massachusetts trial was alleged "lawbreaking" by the CIA in Central America. The jury found the defendants "not guilty." In doing so, it sanctioned a notion of civil disobedience in a democratic society that turns the legitimate concept on its head, a topsy-turvy notion that was the ostensible justification of campus disrupters in the Vietnam era.

Leaving aside the very questionable clarity and proximity of the dangers presented by U.S. foreign policy in Central America to the University of

Massachusetts, respect for the rule of law in a democratic society mandates that if one breaks the law from a motivation of high conscience, one should be prepared to accept, and not evade, the sanctions of the law. In the democratic ethic, we recognize that people of conscience might break the law and willingly suffer the penalty in order to draw attention to an immoral law or state of affairs. There is a long history in democratic societies illustrating this respect. Examples run from Socrates drinking hemlock (despite not being guilty of the charges brought against him) to Martin Luther King, Jr. and his followers filling the jails of the segregationist South.

The logic of the alternative, endorsed by the Massachussets jury, is a society in which the self-proclaimed righteous conscience of any individual, group or mob reigns supreme over democratic process and the rule of law. This sums up the ethic of much of the "movement" that changed American colleges in the late 1960s and early 1970s: the ends justify the means. And it does not matter how questionable the means. In the University of Massachusetts case, the means involved denying campus visitors freedom of speech, as well as disrupting the school's lawful activities.

Another example was given in the spring of 1989 at Queens College of the City University of New York (CUNY), where I am a professor. The State Legislature of New York had voted for a small increase in tuition at CUNY to partially make up for state cuts in funding of the university. At Queens College and several other schools of CUNY, a vocal minority of students went on a raucous "strike" against classes, marching through buildings and disrupting classes. The disruptive students got their way, but their's was a Pyrrhic victory, whose cost was imposed on the entire university community. The governor of the state, Mario M. Cuomo, agreed not to increase tuition, but told CUNY to "absorb" the resulting loss of funds. As a result, fewer sections of basic courses are being offered, fewer elective courses are being offered, and classes are much larger. Thus, once again a large university, in fact the third largest university in the United States, was wounded by a self-righteous minority among its constituents who scorn ethical questions of means.

Separation of ends and means is the first of many dualisms we encounter in higher education. Indeed, as we shall see, the plight of higher education today might be characterized as slow torture by a thousand dualisms.

Proclaiming the righteousness of their anti-war and pro-civil rights causes, and the anything but self-evident clarity of the relationship and proximity of those causes to such matters as college governance, curricula and standards, the student disrupters of the Vietnam era piggybacked their demands for radical reforms of colleges onto their righteous causes. The colleges collapsed, and surrendered much of their academic authority and purpose.

Reasons for the surrender of academic authority are two-fold. First is the often cited fact that the very constitution of a deliberative, collegially organized institution is not well suited for combatting the kinds of unreasoning, raucous, outrageous, vile ("mind-blowing"), physically intimidating and even violent confrontations imposed by the disrupters. This is undoubtedly true. Still, the constitution of the colleges was not the only critical factor. Second, and far more decisive, was the fact that many professors, administrators and trustees were so unsure or unknowing about academic authority that they were intellectually and morally incapacitated in defending learning and the learned. Academic authority was also poorly understood and therefore poorly respected in the larger American society, as it is still.

The separation of "merely" the "process" of reasoned, civil discourse and deliberation from "moral" goals or ends was a trademark of many supporters of the Vietnam era campus disrupters. It is still in vogue, judging from the uncritical, nostalgic treatment of Abby Hoffman's career following his suicide by drug overdose in April 1989. "He helped end the war in Vietnam," was the motif of the press and broadcast media, "through his use of street theater." The latter term, of course, was a 1960s euphemism for disrupting the processes of rational, civil discourse. Such discourse is not a matter of mere "manners," or of "bourgeois politeness."

Civil discourse is an essential requirement for obtaining reasoned decisions in any institution, be it educational or political. The "manners," if you will, of reasoned, civil discourse are absolutely essential to democracy. Unless, of course, one takes the position that a moral elite has the one and only true moral illumination and the one and only true moral position on a question and, therefore, no reasoned discourse or deliberation is necessary. This, as we shall see, was precisely the position of the counterculture movement and of much of the New Left movement, both of which so devastated campuses.

In addition, it goes almost without saying that there was no relating of Hoffman's role in championing the casual use of drugs as a new "life style," to the plague of drugs the nation suffers on and off campuses today as a consequence of counterculturists like Hoffman who counselled the young of the 1960s and 1970s to "tune in, drop out, and turn on."

In the academic year 1968-1969, I was a visiting associate professor of philosophy at City College of New York (CCNY), a college of the City University of New York (CUNY). In that year, the closing of CCNY was forced by a handful of students who cited as their motivation their objections to the admissions policy of CUNY. The policy was to accept only those applicants with the very best high school academic records. Competition was fierce for the tuition-free, high-quality education offered— CCNY had for decades been called "the Harvard of the poor." As a result, the senior colleges of CUNY admitted only freshman who had excelled in high school, a small percentage of the total number of applicants, and these included few blacks. Demands were made for open admissions and the admission of many more blacks. That year some students decided to advance the demands by forcibly closing the college.

Until then, the classes I taught in political philosophy and in ethics had discussed basic issues involved in the CUNY admissions controversy— e.g., democratic process, equity, equality, authority, social justice—in the light of readings I assigned from such authors as Plato, Kant, Rousseau, Hobbes, Locke, the *Federalist* papers, Marx, Marcuse, Dewey and Hook.

Suddenly, one morning, in a planned action, some students blocked the few and relatively narrow entrances to CCNY's South Campus, pushing back anyone who sought to go through their lines. Estimates of the numbers of students who closed the large college varied, but in my observation they never totalled more than 300. The overwhelming majority of students wanted classes to continue, and the college had every right to conduct classes. Amid much confusion, disturbance, emotional discussion in the press and on television in New York City, and emergency deliberation by CUNY's governing board (appointees of the governor of the State of New York and the mayor of New York City), some classes continued.

Intimidation at this point turned to violence—how much violence is still a controversial point. I witnessed some, in particular the rough man-handling of a professor about sixty years of age. He protested to students attempting to block the passage of students and faculty in the corridors of Stiegliz Hall, in which the offices and most classes of the philosophy department were housed. He told them that the disruptions were like those in German universities in the early period of Hitler's rule. At this point, some of the disrupters began "playfully" to push him hard from one to another as if the man were a basketball. After a long moment of shocked and fearful paralysis on the part of the large number of onlookers, almost all of them students, a number of us went to the professor's aid, attempting to extricate him from his assaulters. We did so, in a mass shoving melee, and I saw several students exchange flurries of punches.

CUNY's Board closed CCNY, but in time an opposing group obtained a court order reopening the school. Classes resumed just before the end of the semester, with New York City police stationed in the halls of the college's buildings.

Recently, I've told the story of the "student strike" at CCNY and of other student disruptions at Columbia, where students urinated from upper story windows on police called to restore order on the campus after college buildings were seized and files and equipment were destroyed; at Cornell, where students carried guns onto the campus to force their demands upon the university; and of even worse violence and disruption on other campuses, including the bombings of laboratories and other buildings.

Today's young students listen politely to the accounts of these events that took place at about the time some of them were born, or afterward. It is news to them. They are a generation that has read little of the major events of history, let alone history's details. Some express astonishment that such things could have happened, but none of them asks about the basic issues that were involved. They seem uninterested in tracing the effects and lessons of the campus history of twenty or twenty-five years ago on the colleges they are attending and the education they are receiving. I told them of a faculty member in the early 1970s at Queens College who screamed "Don't listen to them! Don't trust any of them!" to a group of students protestors to whom a college dean was attempting to speak. Not one of today's students asked "Why?"

The faculties on American campuses are quiet, in fact extremely reluctant to talk about what happened. Their reluctance is matched by foundations which support much research by academics. In June 1987, the University Centers for Rational Alternatives reported that it had surveyed grants for educational research given by major foundations since 1975. It found that:

> Despite the fact that billions of dollars were distributed to underwrite tens of thousands of projects, we have not been able to discover a single grant of any significance made for a scholarly study of the

violent disruptions of American academic life that altered so radically the academic landscape of the nation.

The reluctance by faculty to examine the Vietnam period and its continuing effects on colleges stems from a mixture of motives. "We all have to live with each other," it is said. Some faculty are ashamed of their inaction in defense of the authority of learning and the institutions and profession dedicated to it in the face of the assaults and dangers of the time. They would rather the period not be raised at all. "We are a group made up of people who by inclination and training are suited to contemplation and deliberation, not confrontation and struggle," it is often said. And when I wrote in a publication of the American Association of University Professors in February 1986 that only some faculty in the U.S. attempted actively to defend "authentic academic traditions" during the Vietnam period's assaults on them, a faculty member wrote in response, dismissing the defenders as "reactionaries."

Whatever the mixture of motives, the reluctance to analyze the most turbulent period in American higher education, when it was most effectively changed, would condemn us to learn little or nothing from the experience. It requires examination because of the claims it made, explicitly and implicitly, about education, culture and democracy. It also calls for examination because we are living both with the results of the activity and with simultaneous attempts to continue and expand those effects as well as attempts to "reverse" many of them.

Unfortunately, as we shall see, the efforts to preserve the radical changes of the 1960s and 1970s and the efforts at counterreform in other directions since the 1980s are, paradoxically, *both* fundamentally antipathetic to authentic academic traditions. The authority of learning and of the learned was hurricaned by the winds from the social and political New Left in the late 1960s and early 1970s, and are being overwhelmed (albeit much less violently or conspicuously) by commercialist winds today. Neither camp is interested in the unique essence of higher education—freedom of learning, the authority of learning, and their *sine qua non* relationship to an open, free, democratic society. In fact, the New Left was and remains rabidly hostile to the academic ethos, and the powerful, commercialist reform forces of today are indifferent to, or contemptuous of, the academic ethos.

What must be understood is how the alterations of higher education forced by the New Left twenty years ago are in theory and practice not just an historical aberration. They were not the results of student inanities comparable to the panty raids of the 1950s or the gold fish swallowing of the 1920s. Nor were they just the temporary effects of a mad time or peculiar circumstances in history (the Vietnam War and the climax of the civil rights movement). They were, and remain, nothing less than a claim on and challenge to the very soul of higher education.

As is still its wont, the New Left seized upon certain "good causes" as justification of its assault on colleges and universities. It emphasized grievances and frustrations felt by many about American society at large, and "brought them home" to the schools of higher learning. Institutions in the U.S.—political, governmental, social, economic, religious—were seen, and still are seen, by many non-ideologically oriented Americans, as archaic, inadequate to human needs of our time. They are perceived as being paralyzed by the very bureaucracies that form their corps, and upon which they depend. The bureaucracies seem to act in imperious disregard of the individual, and seem to be impervious to reform from within or without.

New Leftists cast colleges in this mold. The very "slowness" of the colleges to reform, stemming from their nature as deliberative bodies with collegially exercised authority, was and is scored as evidence of their institutional arteriosclerosis and used to whip up frenzy against them. It is telling that the "student strike" which closed CCNY occurred *after* CUNY's Board had announced it was going to change its admissions policies over a timetable of some four years.

Similarly, the "free speech movement" disrupted the University of California at Berkeley in 1964 before the American involvement in the Vietnam War heated up to provide a rationalization for "trashing" higher education. It was led by a physics-major undergraduate who dropped out ostensibly in the cause of a "right" to use obscene language on campus, a cause whose importance and urgency are even more dubious than its justice. (A footnote: That student, Mario Savio, received his bachelor's degree *summa cum laude* in physics in 1984 from San Francisco State University. At commencement, Savio was named the outstanding science student of his graduating class. Mr. Savio has apparently redeemed his education. Redemption of higher education from the chronic crisis caused by him and others is not so easily achieved.)

The uniqueness of the collegial structure was held in contempt by the New Leftists, was derided as reactionary sham, and exploited as a vulnera-

21

ble point of attack. In fact, it was their primary target. A member of the New Left campus movement was quoted in the *New York Times* as early as 5 May 1968 as saying:

Do you know why the demonstrations and protest movements succeeded? Because we did not play by the rules of the game. Our movement wasn't organized democratically. We kicked the Dow people off campus though they had every right to be there. It was our unrepressed intolerance and thorough anti-permissiveness that brought our actions success.

The danger that the assault on the reasoning, noncentralized nature of the colleges might cause the destruction of this very nature, which to a very damaging and critical degree did in fact occur, may have been lost on the callow student followers of the leftist leaders. But the leaders themselves knew better, and sought the destruction as part of their avowed ideology of destroying the nation's (and the colleges') basic structure, which they saw as evil—roots, trunk, branches and leaves. The rationale of the leaders, as they explained repeatedly in the many opportunities given to them by omnipresent TV cameras, was, "This society is rotten! Let's tear it down! Its replacement will emerge from the revolution itself." (Frequently used expletives deleted.)

The zealous irrationality of the New Leftists proved once again what the world learned from the French Revolution. A revolutionary movement need not have a clear ideological goal or even a coherently expressed program to create terror and destruction. Which is to state in another form a truism: The more extreme an irrationality is, the greater its drive, until it reaches its logical end—madness. So in the late 1960s, two professors of drama at Fairleigh Dickinson University in New Jersey ordered the students in their classes to change their allegedly "racist" attitudes or receive failing grades.

Unlike the Communist Old Left of the 1930s, the campus activists of the Vietnam War period did not have a coherently expressed utopia which they offered as the eventual goal of their revolution. Hence, it is no surprise that insofar as they succeeded on campuses, they've left not so much reform as collapse. Robbespierre, their counterpart of another century, exemplified the chaotic revolutionary mind in his last speech before he went to the guillotine in 1794 in the reign of terror he helped bring about and lead.

"We shall perish," he said, "because, in the history of mankind, we missed the moment to found freedom."

The ideological center of the New Left was based not on the Marxist ideal of a Communist society, or on any clear goal, but on a peculiar ideology of human nature. Although its leaders were less than philosophical, or even coherent, we can construct their ideology from what they said and did. It was a pale reflection of Rousseauean philosophy of human nature and of society.

Rousseau held that human nature in "pure" form is good and is free. It becomes evil and enslaved by social institutions, by civilization *as such*. So in *Emile*, Rousseau expressed his premise in terms of the educational and cultural philosophy he developed from it, which had echoes in the anti-education counterculture expressions of the New Left:

All things are good as they come out of the hands of their Creator, but every thing degenerates in the hand of man....He is not content with any thing in its natural state, not even with his own species. His very offspring must be trained up for him like a horse in the menage, and be taught to grow after his own fancy, like a tree in his garden.

And in his *Social Contract*, Rousseau began with a famous statement that sums up the angry mood, and the intellectual perspective of the political thrust of the 1960s' movement, which had no view developed enough to be called "intellectual." "Man is born free," Rousseau wrote, "and everywhere he is in chains." His solution to the political problem was a revolutionary one in which humankind's natural rights are protected and expressed in a process which depends on sovereignty resting in the "general will" (*volonte generale*) of the people. However this is *not* the same as mere majority will, or even unanimous will (*volonte de tous*). The general will expresses the natural, common interests of humanity, while majority will, and even unanimous will, often expresses nothing but a collection of the private, anti-natural desires of individuals. And the general will must be exercised directly, not by representation.

Rosseau's ideas were later repeated, albeit more banally, in the New Left's call for "participatory democracy" which in some vague way (which was not spelled out by Rousseau either, constituting a major flaw in his philosophy) would lead to morally correct political policies, not necessarily those of the majority. The New Left also echoed Rousseau's rejection of representational democracy, in this case that of the United States. As Rousseau put it:

Sovereignty, for the same reason as makes it inalienable, cannot be represented; it lies essentially in the general will, and will does not admit of representation: it is either the same, or other; there is no intermediate possibility. The deputies of the people, therefore, are not and cannot be its representatives: they are merely its stewards, and can carry through no definitive acts. Every law the people has not ratified in person is null and void—is, in fact, not a law.

Rousseau never answered the central question of how the elusive general will was to be determined or expressed—it remained a mystery in his philosophy. The best he offered was the opinion that if the natural potentialities of humankind were left undisturbed by society, a morally good, natural state of affairs would develop.

On the other hand, the New Left's solution of "participatory democracy" in practice turned out to be mob rule, by whatever mob captured the attention of a campus, city or the nation on any given day. Of course, the potential for an individual or group to manipulate such participatory democracy constitutes a demagogue's dream, and there was no lack of demagogues on campuses and elsewhere in the Vietnam period.

Rousseau never gave a clear meaning to what he meant by "nature." He used the word sometimes in ways which suggested empiricism, that human life should be developed through knowledge gained through the senses. At other times, he seems to hint at a pantheistic meaning of the term, the view that nature is coextensive and identical with God. The New Left's answer, on the other hand, was to leave the natural goodness of human nature to its own totally free expressions of instincts and emotions, that is, counterculture. Counterculture was to "green," or make "natural," American education and American culture.

The strong appeal of counterculture was to unexamined and undeveloped emotion, not intellect. Perhaps the closest thing to a coherent expression of it lay in the widespread interpretation, or misinterpretation, of William Goldings's novel *Lord of the Flies* and the film made of it. Both of these were enormously popular with young people in the 1960s and 1970s. This despite the fact that Golding's novel is a highly *critical* reflection on undeveloped emotion at work. Indeed, the novel continues to be popular among young people today, especially among high school students, who paradoxically turn to careerist preoccupations in their college years. The attitude they developed seems to be that if society, or people, are irredeemably corrupt, then one should get lots of money and make the most of living rich in a sour world.

Golding's story of shipwrecked English schoolboys who turn to primitive savagery in their efforts to establish social structures has Rosseauean overtones, at least as viewed by counterculturists of the 1960s and their younger, self-oriented, materialistically prone successors today.

An evaluation of counterculture's capture of higher education is served by an examination of one of its early "positive" expressions. By looking at it we can see not only its "philosophy" but also its psychological appeal, an appeal that is far from gone even among today's more materialistic and "conservative" students, not to mention those faculty and administrators who were themselves protesting students in the Vietnam period and who look back at the era through lenses of biased nostalgia.

In that period, the James Joyce Memorial Theater "did its thing" late at night at the Guggenheim Museum in New York City. In its "playbill," the group claimed to aim at fulfilling a need, the expression of which it attributed to Bertolt Brecht, for "a type of theater which not only releases the feelings, insights, and impulses possible within the particular historical field of human relations in which the action takes place, but employs and encourages those thoughts and feelings which help transform the field itself." It is a statement not dissimilar to the aims of the campus activists toward their colleges.

In the James Joyce Liquid Theater, the "audience" (about 300 people, of whom I was one) were gently led through a series of exercises with others in shifting groups by the "cast" (about twenty-five young adults). The exercises were of four kinds: 1. physical exercises of kinds familiar to dancers and athletes—head rolling, bending, shoulder-flexing, etc.; 2. non-verbal communication exercises of the type known to every one familiar with acting classes or parlor games—"Say hello to your partner with your eyes"; 3. exercises borrowed from encounter groups popular in the 1960s—"Listen to your partner's body" (heartbeat, pulse, breathing); 4. group movements superficially akin to religious rituals and dance—moving circles of hand-holding people, humming in unison.

The one point in the two-and-one-half hour evening in which the "cast" resorted to putting on a play for the audience consisted of a fifteen minute pantomime skit by two actors on man's creation and his discovery of his sexuality. It was uncreative, infantile and dull, as was the original music played during the evening.

At best, the Liquid Theater was mildly relaxing. For the most part, it was boring. Boring because it was empty of those things that make for theater—personality of playwright, director and actors, professional skills, developed characters, story, thoughts and feelings. It was all too typical of the expressions of counterculture, including those on campuses. In its efforts to reform, it threw out the essence.

In its efforts to reform important institutions, including higher education, counterculture succeeded most in dissipating life, literally creating nothing where before there had been something, however flawed. The dissipation continues to this day in a persistent fallacy of counterculture entrenched in the minds of people on campuses and elsewhere. That is the belief that "consciousness" constitutes understanding, creativity, love, morality, and educational, political and social agendas, or all of these. In fact, it does not constitute any of them.

People went to the Liquid Theater expecting something profound, or in the patois of the time, something "heavy." They then deluded themselves that they had found it. They succumbed to the great temptation, the perhaps most longed-for wish in our often cold, confused and dangerous world—instant meaning. Instant understanding and instant love were to be had, without bother of time, courage or effort to get to know and care. Instant community was at hand, without hard, lengthy efforts at intellectual, spiritual and practical tasks which create community as their by-product.

Turning to, and against, colleges, instant education was the reform, with no study, no skills developed, standards held and sought, no structured content, and none of the difficulties involved in learning—conceiving, gathering, organizing and testing ideas and information, knowledge and opinion. Except for emphasis on feelings about feelings, akin to static on a radio, the education advanced by counterculture was empty of understanding and real feeling. It was literally *nothing*, except perhaps getting into the habit of vile behavior. If there was a "culture" in counterculture, it was simply vileness.

It is little surprise that a 1985 study by the Cooperative Institutional Research Program of the University of California at Los Angeles of

182,000 college freshmen at 345 colleges, the inheritors of the legacy of counterculture, found them to be "materialistic," but not "conservative" or anything else which would give them a positive identification beyond the money they hope to make.

In fact 57.4 percent of the students called themselves politically "middle of the road," and more said they were "liberal" or "far left" than those labelling themselves politically "conservative" or "far right." An all-time high, 22 percent of them, planned to go into business careers, while an all-time low percentage of them intended to go into the performing arts. Some 70 percent of them answered that "being very well off financially" was a primary goal, up from about 38 percent in 1970. Only about 44 percent rated "developing a meaningful life philosophy" as a primary goal, down from 85 percent in 1968.

A study of undergraduates in all class standings done in 1986 by the Carnegie Foundation found both that college students are generally "satisfied" with the [disjointed, incoherent and shallow] education they are receiving, and that paradoxically, that same education "bores" 37 percent of them. About 41 percent said that if they were given the choice of a good job they would drop out of college at once and take it. The "yuppie" ideal in our society in general is at once both a determiner and a product of our college education today. And we have gone from mindless yippie to shark-minded yuppie in the blink of an historical eye. Indeed, by ripping out the reasoning heart of higher education, yippies made the student ranks of colleges safe for yuppies.

Counterculture was, strictly speaking, not a new culture. It was anticulture. Notwithstanding its anti-intellectualism and its emphasis on sentience and immanence, it was not a mystical culture or even a sensual one. It was crude irrationalism, a know-nothingism, as distinct from a nonrational religion such as Buddhism. It was a nonculture whose members were not the "holy barbarians" they fancied themselves to be, but quite simply and plainly barbarous in that they lacked any culture. The thrust of this barbarism was counterculture's frantic pursuit of paradise, coupled with the self-delusion that the usually banal results of the pursuit indeed constituted paradise.

The counterculture *Paradiso* was often termed "The Woodstock Nation." In 1969, the immersion of 400,000 people in mostly crude music distorted by monstrous ear-assaulting amplifiers, in rain, mud and sex play for three days at Woodstock was praised as the highest and most noble

27

human experience in modern times. The chaos, banality, filth, drug intoxication and drug psychosis that marked it—all of this was defended with a vociferousness that is incredible unless one understands the psychology driving it.

The Woodstock Nation was not a community, nor was it sensual or loving. It was a mass, chaotic indulgence in sentimentality, feeling *about* something rather than actually experiencing it. It was an ignorant and immature indulgence in *notions* of love, sensuality and community that blotted out reality. Tolstoy told of sentimental, aristocratic Russian women who went to the theater and shed copious tears stimulated by maudlin plays about human suffering, while their coachmen outside froze in the winter cold. Except with the counterculturists, it was their own humanity they neglected and degraded as well as that of others. Their less than casual human relations blotted out any depth or caring. And their self-proclaimed "Christ-like" and "Buddha-like" sham of mysticism destroyed any sense of, or zest in, human concerns or accomplishments beyond transient tinglings in their own nervous systems. Their drug reliance did not merely pass time, but *killed* time, not in the sense of a mystical religious transcendence of time, but in the sense that intoxication, psychosis and death kill time.

More important today, the "drug culture" encouraged and glamorized by counterculture leaders was a major cause of the terrible drug scourge that afflicts American society today. Today's plague of crack, cocaine, angel dust and heroin are directly traceable to the counterculture's wild propaganda and proselytizing for LSD, mescaline, amphetamines and marijuana. That many of the counterculture leaders did not know how dangerous drugs are to individuals, culture and society is an excuse that one hears today. It won't wash. Some of the world's cultures have had centuries of experience with drugs, e.g., the use of hashish in North Africa. Much could have been learned by studying that experience. Counterculture leaders, a supremely anti-intellectual, anti-learning group, were not interested in learning. Indeed they mocked and spat on the very idea. They were not shy in proclaiming their intention to destroy culture and society—higher education being foremost among their targets. Looking back from the drug-tormented society and diminished higher education of today, we must give the counterculturists their due. They had an enormous degree of success in fulfilling their intention. For us today to avoid learning the lessons of the counterculture experience because of some too tender reluctance to engage in recrimination against some of our colleagues, or ourselves, is to continue the mad counterculture ideal of stubbornly held, deliberate ignorance.

Nothingness was counterculture's ultimate value. Nietzche termed nihilism "the most gruesome of guests," and such was the nature of the force brought by the guests who changed colleges in the 1960s and 1970s—the counterculture activist students who passed through the schools, and their allies among the faculty, administrations and their off-campus allies. It largely explains why colleges now greatly reflect counterculture. The more overtly political arm of the New Left had considerable success in tearing down higher education, and its counterculture arm replaced the old with...nothingness. Perhaps there is something to the overused psychoanalytic cliché that every case of self-destruction (suicide) is but the inward turning of outwardly directed destructive urges (homicide). Counterculture, while it purported to have had its roots in hatred of war and injustice, turned its destruction against itself in a massive suicide of the mind and spirit. To the considerable extent that colleges merged with counterculture, they shared in that death. It remains to be seen whether higher education can transform the death into a component of a living dialectic that can lead to renewal. That dialectic would parse in the following logic:

Thesis: Higher education's pre-Vietnam out-of-touch reliance on abstract reason (*raison*) and memory as distinguished from broader intelligence; its high degree of formalism, intellectual aridness and rigidity.

Antithesis: The Vietnam period's campus anti-democratic New Left political radicalism and nihilistic counterculture.

Synthesis: A balance of intellectual and esthetic development, meaningful studies, and colleges that are free and have academic authority and contribute to a free society.

Higher education was vulnerable to being turned topsy-turvy because its growth had accelerated exponentially after World War II, and it lost its sense of itself in its preoccupation with the process of managing its growth. In 1910, 274 years after Harvard had opened in 1636, only 4.8 percent of the nation's population between the ages of 18 to 21 was attending college. To be sure, there had been great development of American higher education in the two and three-quarter centuries since 1636. But it had been slow. For most of that time, in fact until the Civil War, higher education was a matter of education for professionals, first for ministers, then others. The president of Yale was both frank and accurate when he said

29

in 1754, "Colleges are Societies for Ministers, for training up persons for the Work of the Ministry." In fact, as late as 1861, 20 percent of college graduates went into the ministry.

Over considerable time, higher education expanded to include training for doctors, lawyers and eventually a handful of the sons of gentlemen farmers and the captains of the merchant trades. Scores of small colleges opened in the U.S. The intent was to train the leaders of American communities. The concept of that leadership was expanded from a handful of professions at first, to the wealthy and genteel classes, then in an ever-widening democratization to the ideal of making the opportunities of higher education available to all classes and groups as sources of potential leaders of society.

The curriculum of colleges was at first narrow, and changed little for a long time, consisting of classical history and literature, ancient languages (Latin and Greek for all, with the addition of Hebrew for divinity students), and, of course, the Bible. In fact, the education Thomas Jefferson and John Adams (at, respectively, the College of William and Mary and Harvard University) and their generation received differed little from what was offered in the Renaissance universities of Europe. It consisted of a fixed body of knowledge, called the "liberal arts," containing eternal truths, to be memorized. These were based on the *Septem Artes Liberales* set in medieval schools, and the literature of the Greco-Roman civilization. Founded on Aristotilian categories of knowledge, the original seven liberal arts were grammar, logic (or dialectics), rhetoric, music, arithmetic, geometry and astronomy. (Not all seven were offered in the revised curricula of the early American colleges, which added Biblical studies and classical literature.)

A struggle to include other subjects was long and slow in gaining ascendancy. Harvard, as early as 1728, established the teaching of modern sciences, and did so by the radically new teaching method of demonstrating experiments for the students.

In 1756, the tiny College of Philadelphia, still devoted to training the leadership of the land, found it necessary that such leaders be educated much more broadly. It introduced a curriculum that was precociously modern. One-third of it was still the traditional study of Latin and Greek. But one-third was given to logic, ethics, metaphysics, history, political science, trade and commerce, and the remaining third consisted of English language and literature. In addition, the study of modern foreign languages was encouraged during the students' "leisure hours."

Thomas Jefferson drew up a plan for the University of Virginia, which opened in 1825, that would have divided the University into separate *schools,* consisting of ancient languages, modern languages, medicine, natural sciences, mathematics and others. It was a plan for professional rather than liberal education—"liberal" meaning free from vocational or other goals except the training of the student's mind and the formation of his character. But the State of Virginia did not implement Jefferson's plan. (Harvard adopted an experimental version of Jefferson's *Virginia Plan* in 1825 that was both pioneering and highly influential on other schools.)

The inclusion of many more subjects than just the classical liberal arts and Christian studies led to what historians John S. Brubacher and Willis Rudy label in their *Higher Education In Transition* (1976) "the central educational battle of nineteenth-century America," the fight for the elective system.

The most influential force in the pre-Civil War liberalization of the curriculum and focus on the needs and preferences of the individual student was the Yale Report of 1827. It called for a balance of required classical studies to give an essential foundation to training the mind and right character, then elective studies in which that training could be focused on a student's choice from a variety of modern subjects.

The most radical proposal of all presaged the situation in the 1980s. In 1850, the president of Brown University proposed that "Every student might study what he chose, and nothing but what he chose." The extremely controversial plan was tried briefly at Brown, then abandoned in the face of criticism that it caused a decline in scholarly standards and in the quality of students at Brown. These objections were, of course, offered in the context of knowledge of a traditional core of learning, the classical liberal arts. And "student quality" referred to the character of students as measured by their ability to speak publicly about the principles of right character as learned in the liberal arts study. As we shall see, today the debate has been renewed in updated, somewhat different terms.

With the Civil War, it was clear that America had begun its change to an industrial and "scientifically" agricultural society. In the midst of the war, in 1863, President Lincoln signed a bill that became the Morrill Act, through which the federal government granted public lands in the frontier areas (the midwest and west) to found public colleges which stressed major studies in the agricultural and mechanical arts. With the Act, higher education was expanded in size and scope. Some public colleges had been founded before then, such as the Free Academy in New York City in 1847, which became the tuition-free City College of New York. But the Morrill Act enabled an eventual major expansion of the public sector of higher education. It led to affordable education for increasing percentages of American families, to the point where today, 75 percent of all college students are enrolled in public colleges.

Although some colleges, such as West Point (founded in 1802), and Rensselaer Polytechnical Institute (founded in 1824), had previously included practical arts, the Morrill Act opened the way to practical education for great numbers of people. By 1900 there were forty-two technological colleges in the U.S., including the Massachussetts Institute of Technology (MIT), which opened in 1865. By 1950 there were 160 engineering colleges alone in the U.S.

In the late nineteenth century, the influence of research-oriented German universities—as distinct from the old Oxford-Cambridge model of training of the mind and character through tutoring in the classical liberal arts —led to the scheme that was to be the standard for most American colleges until the late 1960s. It is usually identified with the one person who was most influential in its adoption, Charles W. Eliot, president of Harvard from 1869 to 1909.

Harvard adopted a plan familiar to us today: 1) required courses were taken mostly in the freshman year; 2) electives, with a few exceptions, could not be taken until required courses were completed; 3) electives were grouped into disciplines and offered by departments; 4) students elected major and minor concentrations of studies from among the disciplines; and 5) most courses were of a half-year duration rather than the standard one-year courses.

An insignificant development of teaching methods and goals paralleled that of the curricula development in the long history to the 1960s. The early goals of higher education, educating leaders of the community by training their minds and forming their characters, was first sought through the recitation method, placing great premium on a student's memory, his ability to absorb the body of absolute knowledge contained in the classical liberal arts and the Bible. This was neatly symbolized in 1815 when the founders of Allegheney College placed in its cornerstone a piece of Virgil's tomb and a piece of Plymouth Rock.

Recitation, a method that dominated 200 years of American higher education, was designed to train a student's mind by "mental exercise." The

32

student had to recite verbatim in class what he had memorized in his assigned reading. He did this on cue from his instructor, the cue usually being the instructor's statement of opening words or lines from the assigned reading.

An exception to the recitation method was the "prelection" used in Catholic colleges by Jesuit instructors. This consisted of exposition and commentary on subject matter by the instructor, followed by the student's demonstration that he had absorbed the lesson by repeating it orally at a later date.

The prelection prefigured the slow, widespread, adoption of the lecture method in the nineteenth century. It was borrowed from Germany as a method of giving students both information and scholarship of the subject matter as brought up to date by research, and formed by the distinctive selection, organization, cast, twist or interpretation given by the individual instructor. From the beginning, the lecture method faced criticism that was to reach an explosive climax in the late 1960s. The students could read the lectures, it was said, instead of furiously taking notes.

The seminar approach—reading followed by discussion between instructor and students as a group—was a reform that has been used less in undergraduate than in graduate education. It requires a low "student-to-instructor ratio" (a professor teaching only a few students in a class), and therefore is expensive. However, there can be little doubt that it is the most effective way to teach most subjects, with few notable exceptions.

Early on, students were tested through the "disputation" method of oral examination upon a topic set by the instructor at "public exhibition." The disputation yielded slowly in the nineteenth century to written examinations, considered more comprehensive. After all, the disputation tested a student's mastery of only one, or at best, very few topics.

At the same time, the changes marked by the Civil War accelerated the growth of higher education for women. In the antebellum period, a number of colleges for women were founded. The practice had to make way against the strong prevailing prejudice that the only education needed by women was that of the finishing school model, which taught women to be, as one author put it, "correct in their manners, respectable in their families, and agreeable in society." And this, of course, was limited only to the daughters of genteel families. In 1851, Catherine Beecher in *The True Remedy for the Wrongs of Women* correctly criticized the "female colleges" as being in fact only high schools at best, falling far short of the standards of the better men's colleges. A departure occurred when

Oberlin College in 1833 became the first true college in the English-speaking world to admit women.

But the post-Civil War transformation of the U.S. saw the acceleration of true higher education for women, with the opening of high quality women's colleges, like Vassar (1865), Wellesley (1875) and others, still, to be sure only for the genteel classes.

By 1900, there were 119 women's colleges in the U.S. Coeducational higher education, on the other hand, was much slower in expanding, becoming almost universal only in the last twenty years. In 1960, there were 300 women's colleges. Thirteen years later, the number dropped by half, and dwindled to 101 in the 1980s, men's colleges also going coeducational in the same period.

Yet in the late 1980s, enrollments at the remaining women's colleges went up—e.g., by 6.6 percent in 1987, according to the Women's College Coalition. Wellesley College President Nannerl Keohane was quoted as saying all-female colleges afford a woman not only "equal opportunity, but every opportunity." A Carnegie Foundation report in 1986 had found that in coed colleges "even the brightest women students often remain silent" in the presence of men. And at all-female colleges, 61 percent of the faculty is female, vs. 27 percent on average at all colleges. Students at all-female colleges frequently report they find their college more nurturing than coed schools.

The inclusion of Roman Catholics, Jews and blacks in higher education came to fruition in the twentieth century, but each followed a long and different route. Before 1900, several colleges for blacks were established in the south, staffed by northern-educated missionaries. Among the early schools were Avery College (1849), Wilberforce (1856), Lincoln (1854), and Moorehouse (1867). With the major emphasis on vocational training, the quality of education they offered was poor and was denounced as such in the early twentieth century by W.E.B. DuBois.

The integration of blacks into white colleges moved slowly but steadily forward so that in 1952 only five state universities, all of them in the south, still excluded blacks. The civil rights movement's climactic thrust following *Brown vs. Topeka* in 1954 not only saw desegregation, but also saw black enrollment in northern colleges more than double from 45,000 in 1954 to 95,000 or 7 percent of total college enrollment by 1970. In 1976, black students made up 9.4 percent of all college students, but by 1987 their percentage declined to 8.8 percent of all students.

Jews, following their mass migration to the United States, which peaked in the first two decades of the twentieth century, were at first excluded or "restricted" in numbers through quotas at many schools. The most significant exceptions were public colleges, in particular the municipal colleges of New York City. The quotas at many private schools were not completely overcome until after World War II.

The history of Roman Catholics in American higher education begins with the founding of Catholic universities, starting with Georgetown in 1789. The integration of Catholics into non-Catholic institutions—the old private colleges initially founded by Protestant denominations, and the newer state colleges stimulated by the Morrill Act—moved against strong know-nothing bigotry and was not accomplished until the twentieth century. The Irish, whose immigration peaked in the nineteenth century, led the way. Other, "more recent" groups, e.g., Poles and Italians, have enrolled in American colleges in appreciable numbers only since the 1960s.

Until the late nineteenth century, teaching was virtually the sole activity of American colleges, following the pattern of Oxford and Cambridge after which U.S. colleges were modelled. The next great qualitative change was the adoption of another model, from Germany, which included the obligation to advance knowledge through research.

The history of American universities as great research centers and graduate schools as well as undergraduate teaching institutions started with the founding of Johns Hopkins *as a university* (with 54 graduate students and only 35 undergraduates) in 1875, and the transformation of liberal arts colleges into universities. For example, Princeton College changed its name to Princeton University in 1896, and Columbia College became Columbia University in 1912. The development of large American universities continued at a relatively slow pace until World War II, then accelerated quickly to the point where there are well over 100 major universities in the U.S. today (again defined by their research activities and graduate schools). In 1918, 562 PhD degrees were granted in the U.S. By 1940, the figure was 3,000. But ten years later, it doubled, and by 1965, 15,000 PhDs were being granted annually by 175 institutions.

Undergraduate enrollment kept the same pace. A steady, but slow growth had seen enrollments in the U.S. rise from 36,480 students, or 4.8 percent of the eighteen to twenty-one year old population in 1910, to 1.4 million, or 15.3 percent of the eighteen to twenty-one year olds in 1940. But by 1960, the number of college students jumped to 3.2 million, representing

33.2 percent of eighteen to twenty-one year olds, and by 1970 it leaped to 8.4 million, with almost half of the college-age population actually attending college—a percentage that held through the 1980s. Today it is joined by the fastest growing segment of the student population, the "nontraditional" student over the age of twenty-five, swelling the student ranks to 12 million (7 million full-time and 5 million part-time).

The peculiarly American story of ever-increasing access to higher education now included an ever-widening diversity of educational offerings in a complex, noncentralized system of colleges. Expansion of the educational enterprise continued and moved slowly to World War II and beyond. Then it exploded in a decade and a half. The stages of that history were: 1) to train leaders in an ever-expanding catalogue of areas; 2) to make opportunities for leadership available to ever-widening segments of the American population; 3) to include many areas of knowledge in the university; and 4) to expand the capacities of the mind from character-formation goals drawn from a fixed body of knowledge to the ability to conceive of the world through several scholarly and scientific disciplines. Since the counterculture upset goals that had evolved over more than 300 years, the efforts at reestablishing higher education today revolve around the basic questions which make up the historical emphases.

As a consequence of the explosive and willy-nilly growth and bewildering complexity of higher education in the post-World War II period, its mission became unsure. Its sense of itself and its purposes became confused, even as demands upon it grew apace with its exploding expansion and great diversification.

We can compare the history of higher education in the U.S. to the life of a person in an ever accelerating time frame. The infancy of higher education in the U.S. had a leisurely 200 years and more to develop to 1860; its childhood developed over the next 100 years; but its adolescence was compressed into a stormy decade and a half between 1965 to 1980. Higher education now faces the challenge of defining its maturity. The adolescence included, however, life-threatening traumas (the turbulence of the 1960s and 1970s), from whose devastation it must recover even as it faces the responsibilities of adulthood.

There is a broad consensus today that higher education needs rehabilitation.

But the foremost, central question asserts itself: What is to be the character of higher education? As it always has, the answer hinges on basic philosophical issues, such as what is human nature and the nature of society, what is the nature of knowledge, and what should be the relationships between human nature, society and knowledge in a democracy. Philosophy may bake no bread, but without it, bread-baking becomes careless, and the bread itself tasteless and unnourishing.

3.

The Paideia of American Higher Education

PAIDEIA IS a Greek term which in broad definition means the particular, deepest character of a civilization and culture as it has developed in history.

America's paideia is multifaceted, defying ready description. But among the strains at the core of the American paideia are the commitment to bring intelligence to bear on human affairs, faithfulness to a democratic ethic, and a robust pluralism with regard to personal and group moralities as long as no behavior violates the democratically achieved law governing all.

Again, this is not the whole of the American character, but it is an essential part of its vital core. All Americans can live with this paideia. Conversely, America will not survive if it is abandoned, at least not as America. This core character is a major part of the foundation of our culture as it has developed in the long course of American history. Although the core is not the whole of the American paideia, it allows all individuals and groups who adhere to certain minimum democratic rules to develop whatever culture, morality, religion, philosophy or "life-style" that appeals to them. It even includes those individuals and groups who hold that the American paideia is wrong and should be restricted or otherwise changed. On the base of this "enabling" core the rest of the American character has been developed and continues to evolve.

The three cited features of the American paideia—disciplined, applied intelligence; loyalty to the democratic ethic; and pluralism—form the paideia of American higher education. It is this character of higher education which needs to be restored.

Formal education is the sum of those processes by which a community deliberately preserves, transmits and develops its own living character, its paideia. When it is vital, education thrives "naturally," as it were, and seeks excellence in terms of that character. This evolution characterized American higher education from the founding of Harvard in 1636 until World War II.

When a community's paideia weakens or stagnates, the character of its institutions marks time by becoming formalistic. In many ways this was true both of the U.S. and of American higher education in the 1950s.

When a community's character is violated to the point of being critically wounded, education loses its meaning and sense of purpose, and becomes spiritually and psychologically depressed—the scenario of American higher education since the mid-1960s.

It is time to reorient ourselves to the authentic American paideia. The foremost means of doing so is to revive and renew the consciousness of, and enthusiasm for, those values which best govern American life through our educational efforts. The alternatives, continued drift or the grafting of a different character onto the American soul are both unacceptable. The first is a prescription for mediocrity, and the second a literal impossibility. Whatever the message of the Frankenstein story and its imitators, souls can no more be transferred from society to society than from individual to individual.

The artificial imposition of an unhistorical, alien or archaic paideia onto the American character (or onto the character of higher education) will not take because it is not the natural result of the living process of cultural development in all of history's concrete reality. Cultural evolution in history can be only violated at the cost of losing its essential spirit. It cannot just be bypassed, not even temporarily. Again, a community's paideia is, and of necessity must be, rooted in its living history. Thus the inevitable result of cultural grafting does nothing to stave off mediocrity and may even advance it by diverting creative efforts into dead-ends.

Suggestions and demands to impose social and economic reforms on American culture by imposing them on the system of higher education abound today. These proposals come from the cultural and political New Left and from the commercialist spectra of American pluralism, even as colleges struggle to overcome their depressed passivity and reform themselves.

It should seem incontrovertible that higher education should be dedicated to the cultivation of a disciplined, free, critical and creative intelligence, and to the application of that intelligence to all areas of human concern. After all, now that the counterculture is a spent force, who is against intelligence?

In fact, free intelligence is not accepted by many, both outside and inside of academia. They contend that intelligence should be subordinated to and made servile to some system of fixed truths, traditions and doctrines—metaphysical, religious, moral, political, economic—or to world views in which are found definite, if not fixed, laws, rules, values, priorities, or urgencies. Freud's definition of the formidable German word *Weltanschauung* covers them all (and is not at all dependent on his specific philosophy):

An intellectual construction which solves all the problems of our existence uniformly on the basis of one overriding hypothesis, which, accordingly, leaves no question unanswered and in which everything that interests us finds its fixed place.

To many parties pressing for reform of higher education today, education is seen as a process of bringing individuals into conformity or "harmony" with a world view, of forming or molding mind and character in accordance with a preferred "true," "traditional," "natural," "real," "genuine," "needed," "historically ordained" or "revolutionary" *Weltanschauung*.

My "modest proposal" is that free intelligence should be a goal of today's reform of higher education. To those who would make intelligence and higher education servile to other ends, it will be even outrageous.

Free intelligence has a recognizable character. The defining characteristics of free intelligence are sets of rules for seeking truth that have developed in the history of intellectual disciplines, and independence from all other authority and goals except its own. Whatever the other ancillary goals of a college education, the central aims should be to cultivate in students the skills and habits of intelligence, an understanding of its rules, and a respect for the authority of intelligent inquiry.

The rules of intelligent inquiry and the types of evidence appropriate to different questions differ. They range from the pure logic of mathematics to the natural sciences' protocols of quantified, empirical evidence and controlled testing with repeatable results, to the social sciences' careful, standardized collection and reasoned interpretation of information, and to the humanities' employment and critique of individualized reason and esthetic skills and norms. One of the marks of the educated mind is the ability to discriminate between the forms of evidence, reason, demonstration and criticism that are appropriate to different genres of questions. No less a rigorous thinker than Aristotle acknowledged this when he admonished that the question of what is good for man cannot be answered with mathematical exactitude, because the nature of the subject matter, human behavior, cannot be determined with mathematical exactitude.

To be sure, there are differences on a philosophical level about which rules and what types of evidence are appropriate to various fields, for example morality and esthetics. Rationalists claim the rules of logic are primary or self-sufficient; empirical knowledge takes a secondary role. Empiricists and naturalists take the converse position. Idealists see the inquiry after truth as the understanding and contemplation of eternal forms, essences or universals. Realists see truth only in the objects of the world, which are thought to have essential existence independent of our experiences of them.

The faculty in a college or university do not need to settle once and for all these perennial questions to maintain a community dedicated to inquiry after truth. The community remains open to the extent it continuously examines the perennial questions, encourages the critical intellectual powers of its members, and places no limits on those powers. The academic community becomes closed to the extent that it limits or neglects the critical intellectual powers in favor of fixed unchanging truths (as with the spiritual heirs of Plato), historical "laws" (as with the various intellectual descendants of Hegel and Marx), divine revelation (as with Christian and other religious orthodoxies), or "practical" urgencies (as with those who see education as primarily training for jobs needed by the U.S. economy, or indoctrination in ideology needed for patriotic vigor).

In contrast, a free intellectual community depends on a continuing discourse about the specific procedures of finding truth in different areas of subject matter, about proofs or testing methods, and about types of evidence admissible in the various disciplines. It depends also on free dissemination and free discussion of specific findings by those trained in the disciplines. The ethos of the university is closed when someone or some group decides these questions for the entire community, regardless of how "moral" or "righteous" the regulators' underlying commitment.

Of course, as would-be regulators never cease to tell us, there is a danger that the present trend toward intellectual drift may lead to nihilism, the attitude that there is no meaning at the ground of anything. On the other hand, the closing of inquiry by sanctifying one method of seeking truth, or enshrining one body of knowledge, stifles both the freedom and spirit of the mind in favor of intellectual work which is merely the endless recapitulation (with perhaps some small elaboration) of "eternal truths," or service in advancing "scientific-historical" "laws," or in meeting "urgent national interests."

Free and open intellectual communities can, and in countless colleges do, easily include many individuals who favor educational servility to ideal forms, historical imperatives, or social-economic needs and trends. A *community* of those dedicated to servility, on the other hand, has a natural distaste, if not hostility, for openness. Such groups often argue for and work toward the yoking of the mind to "true" intellectual service—respectively, strict harmony with absolute truth, the advancement of historical inevitability, or serving the nation by requiring key practical skills and desired values. Those who would "reform" the university into a closed community are highly influential in higher education today. This contested endeavor will be hammered out in the next twenty years or so, during which 80 percent of the aging corps of 500,000 American college faculty will be replaced by new faces.

At this critical time, three forces—the intellectual kin of Plato, Hegel and Babbitt—would turn colleges and universities into closed communities. Although their points of view are very different, absolutists, New Leftists and commercialist/patriotic advocates have common cause in attacking the openness of the university. This common front attack on free intelligence seeks credence by identifying openness with the widely perceived and disapproved current purposelessness on campuses. Their common claim is that there is an inevitable causal relationship between openness and meaningless or "irrelevance." Each camp of the enemies of openness needs to be answered.

In *The Open Society and Its Enemies*, published in 1962, Karl Popper divided the enemies of open societies into two camps. One group is in the broad tradition of Plato, the contemplators of eternal Truths who would work the mind and society into harmony with the Truths. The other group is in the tradition of Hegel, those who would impose their world views on all and insist that the university be made over into an instrument for enacting the imperatives of History.

The latter include the leftist activists on campuses, both of the new and old varieties of leftism. They hold variations on the theme that History is governed by specific laws. The understanding of these laws allows one to prophesy or chart the future. In addition, understanding the laws allows one to advance (it would seem unnecessarily, or at least paradoxically) the course of human endeavors towards accelerating the fulfillment of that prophesy. The momentum of the twenty-five year-old "tradition" of the politicized university, achieved by the New Left, carries the efforts forward today. The current popular good causes of today (replacing the once handy Vietnam War and legal racial segregation in the U.S.) are identified as apartheid in South Africa; U.S. policy in Central America; racial, economic and gender justice in the U.S.; and nuclear disarmament. These causes, it is asserted, require that American higher education and the American intellect be politicized, i.e., be brought to heel.

The answer to Hegel's spiritual children remains that however good the causes, the turning of higher education into activism for political or moral goals restricts freedom of the mind and leaves students' minds largely undeveloped. The taking of political stances by the university violates the intellectual freedom of faculty and students by committing them to political positions as opposed to freely given and self-initiated individual expression, and violates the individual professor's or student's right to remain silent on any, and even on *all,* political issues.

Among Plato's spiritual heirs, the differing advocates of eternal truths, Allan Bloom has emerged in his 1987 book *The Closing Of The American Mind,* as the most intellectually formidable and the most influential. (Other eternal truth advocates, although in some cases politically or economically powerful and thus dangerous to the open university, fall into less intellectually potent and even anti-intellectual camps. For example, the ever-present Christian fundamentalists see intellectual inquiry as subordinate to Biblical revelation. Their challenge is more political than intellectual. Their citations of the Bible are an appeal to authority, not to the intellect.)

Bloom's *The Closing of the American Mind* tangles three thrusts which require separation if his ideas and recommendations are to be evaluated. The *first* consists of a number of criticisms of contemporary American culture and higher education. Many will agree with these criticisms although they may want to qualify at least some of Bloom's absolute judgments. Absolutism is Bloom's frank position. Some other of Bloom's judgments require more dissent than mere qualification. The critical point with regard to all of Bloom's judgments is that one may agree with many of them in whole or part without subscribing to the main philosophical thesis of Bloom's book. In fact, people of many philosophies share some of his criticisms of today's culture and education.

Bloom's *second* and underlying thesis is an advocacy of rationalistic natural law philosophy. "Natural laws" are those rules governing the fundamental order of things which are discoverable through the use of reason alone unaided by experience of other types of inquiry. Bloom does not acknowledge the well-known objections to this tradition of philosophy and the problems with it, let alone answer them. But it is necessary to raise them because Bloom's *third* and most important thesis is that American culture, higher education and democracy should be made to conform to rationalistic natural law philosophy.

The subtitle of Bloom's book is "How Higher Education Has Failed Democracy and Impoverished The Souls of Today's Students." The types of culture, education and democracy Bloom advocates are only vaguely spelled out in his book, especially the "democracy," in marked contrast to the sharpness of his criticisms. But careful scrutiny reveals Bloom's ideas of democracy, culture and education bear a closer resemblance to the anti-democratic premise found in Plato's *Republic,* a work cited repeatedly by Bloom, than to the American democracy which Bloom says he would like "restored."

Bloom's advocacy of rationalistic natural law and a society made to conform to it are carried along by his cutting, acerbic, sometimes telling, and sometimes sour criticisms of today's American scene. We must be careful to distinguish between these criticisms, many of which are popular, and the philosophy they purport to serve.

Among the criticisms that are easy to cheer, even if in many cases it is necessary to discount their absolutism or outrageous overstatement, are:

...Rock music's "three great lyrical themes [are]: sex, hate and a smarmy, hypocritical version of brotherly love." Bloom is right on target with much of rock music when he characterizes all of it as banal ("The unconscious has been made conscious...and what have we found? Mick Jagger tarting it up on the stage..."), and when he characterizes the people in the rock music industry as venal. And there is considerable truth to his major point, which is not the simple moralism we often hear about rock music: "None of this contradicts [students] going about the business of life, attending classes and doing assignments for them. But the [students'] meaningful life is with the music....My concern here is not with the moral effects of this music—whether it leads to sex, violence or drugs. The issue here is its effect on education, and I believe it ruins the imagination of young people and makes it very difficult for them to have a passionate relationship to the art and thought that are the substance of liberal education." In fact, rock music encourages a sense of rebellion against parental and other authority in a psychological process normal among adolescents. But rock music goes on to nurture a sense of self-righteousness among young people about their "superior" values. "Selfishness thus becomes indignation and then transforms itself into morality."

....Much of higher education today is characterized by "trendiness, mere popularization and lack of substantive rigor." And some colleges, departments, and professors resemble "carnival barkers" who pander to students by offering faddish courses Bloom terms "sideshows."

...Today's generation of college students are characterized by careerism and avarice. And careerist education is pushing liberal education into eclipse.

...In the New Left's assault on colleges in the 1960s and 1970s "the community of scholars proved to be no community. There was no solidarity in defense of the pursuit of truth."

..."Humanities languish, but this proves only that they do not suit the modern world. It may very well be the indication of what is wrong with modernity." As a member of the New York Council for the Humanities (which distributes federal grant money) since April of 1984, I have been appalled by how few of the applications the Council receives have any substantial humanities content. Many deal with contemporary social and political issues and are dressed up by savy applicants to appear to examine the issues from the perspectives of the humanities.

...Americans generally and college faculty and students in particular have been "liberated from all the conventional attachments to religion, country, and family," as well as the traditional values of Western civilization which found great cultural expressions in the humanities which students no longer study or value. Thus "a young person today, to exaggerate only a little, actually begins *de novo*, without the givens or imperatives that he would have had only yesterday....He can now choose, but he finds he no longer has a sufficient motive for choice that is more than whim, that is binding."

...Bloom rails against today's cult of the "self," what might be termed the Yuppiezation of America, and the concomitant loss of the American sense of *polity*. "We are social solitaries....the concern with self-development, self-expression, or growth, which flourished as a result of the optimistic faith in a preestablished harmony between such a concern and a society or community, has gradually revealed itself to be inimical to community." "The modern economic principle that private vice makes public virtue has penetrated all aspects of daily life in such a way that there seems to be no reason to be a conscious part of civic existence." "Students will want to get ahead and live comfortably. But this life is as empty and false as the one they left behind. The choice is not between quick fixes and dull calculation. This is what liberal education is meant to show them. But as long as they have the Walkman on, they cannot hear what the great [Western] tradition has to say. And, after its prolonged use, when they take it off, they find they are deaf."

...In our universities, "The relations between natural science, social science and humanities are purely administrative and have no substantial intellectual content," not in theory, in the curricula, or in the relations of faculty to each other.

Many others of Bloom's judgments provoke levels of dissent far deeper than mere demur from his exaggeration and unqualified criticisms. Some are very dubious, fatally flawed, or just plain wrong. Some examples:

...Bloom's often repeated theme that the sublimation of economic want and sexual desire are necessary to the creation of great art, and America by permitting satisfaction of sexual drive and raising its people above poverty has become a nation incapable of producing art. "Thus we demystify economy and sexuality, satisfying their primary demands, taking away what our philosophy tells us is their creative impulse." One, Bloom begs the question of whether the U.S. is producing art. Two, consistent with his very frank disdain for contemporary empirical and behavioral sciences, he presents no evidence, apart from references to Freud's non-empirical theory of sublimation and Nietzsche's dogma that the production of art requires "semen in the blood," to demonstrate that all great artists had to or did in fact live in poverty and/or in sexual abstinence.

...Bloom is right when he draws an analogy between the politicaliza-

47

tion of the German university with the advent of the Nazi era and the assault of the campus radicals of the 1960s and 1970s on the American university. He goes on to explain, "No longer believing in their higher vocation, both gave way to a highly ideologized student populace. And the content of the ideology was the same—value commitment. The university had abandoned all claim to study or inform about value—undermining the sense of the value of what it taught, while turning over the *decision* about values to the folk, the *Zeitgeist*, the relevant." But Bloom takes the parallel too far. "Value commitment" was the parallel *form* of the assaults on higher education in Hitlerian Germany and New Left America; the two were not identical in "content." Bloom is wrong in concluding that "The New Left in America was a Nietzcheanized-Heideggerianized Left."

The thought of both Nietzsche and Heidegger contain many diverse, vague, ambiguous and confused strains. Part of what Bloom means by citing Heidegger is evident in his Rectorial Address of 1933 at the University of Freiburg in which he endorsed Nazism and cited German youth as the nation's authority. It was a complete abdication of moral and academic authority. "The time for decision," Bloom quotes from the Address, "is past. The decision has already been made by the youngest part of the German nation."

Yet Bloom also alludes to that existentialist aspect of Heidegger's thought that glorifies commitment *as such*. But existentialism was not the stance of the New Left. The likes of Rap Brown, Mario Savio, Benjamin Spock, Abbie Hoffman and Jerry Rubin tormented unto death by existential *angst* vis-á-vis the dreadful face of metaphysical nihilism is a premise that Woody Allen would love. The *content* of the New Left's commitment was Hegelian neo-Marxism and a Rousseauean-romantic cult of youth righteousness. These were at the heart of the New Left, not commitment as such. Neither the political radicals or the hippies of the New Left were driven by Heidegger's or Nietzsche's obsession with staving off nihilism. That obsession is Bloom's.

By invoking Nietzsche, Bloom means to show him as a man who proposed antidotes to the nihilism into which he saw the Western world falling, and which Bloom sees reflected in the positivism of the social sciences in both pre-Hitler German and pre-Vietnam U.S. universities. ("Positivism" is the position that there are no ways of gaining any knowledge except through the empirical sciences.)

In all this, Bloom's overstatements border on committing the logical fallacy of the undistributed middle. (An example of which is: Humans are two-legged creatures. Birds are two-legged creatures. Therefore humans are birds.) To say Nazi students in 1933 and American New Left students in 1968 both favored "value commitment" and therefore are all but identical is to rely on the same kind of illogic.

The New Left is best explained not by Nietzsche's and Heidegger's horror at the spectre of nihilism, as Bloom would have it, but by neo-Marxism, which formed the the movement's political edge, strictly speaking, and Rousseau, who gave expression to the notions that underlay its mass counterculture expression by the campus disrupters of the late 1960s and early 1970s. Both Hegel and Rousseau predate modern social science, and their stances had flooded reservoirs of popular thought before the 1960s, reservoirs that were tapped when the Vietnam War and the climax of the civil rights movement gave excuse for their expression.

Neo-Marxism is a simplistic but extremely popular scheme in the world today. It has been very successfully used by some Third World leaders, and by some apologists for the Third World in the U.S. And the USSR has exploited it in the Third World. Many Third World leaders have found it especially useful in their own countries to hold the loyalties of their people, arouse their nationalisms, and scapegoat the West for their own failures. It is as easily schematized as it has been wonderfully useful to those everywhere who hate the West and who hate the Western invention of the democratic, open society.

Thesis: Western Imperialism.

Antithesis: Third World Revolution (of which Vietnam was presented as a heroic example during the student disruptions).

Synthesis: A "just" new world order.

In other countries, Hegelian neo-Marxism and Rousseaueanism did not have the excuses of war in Vietnam and Bull Connor in Alabama, and did not need them. There were violent student demonstrations all over the world in the 1960s and 1970s. Those which claimed the most lives took place in Mexico, a nation which did not have a single soldier in Vietnam. Also, Mexico did not have a a Nietzschean-Heideggerian dread of nihilism in Western civilization. But Mexico did have political and economic problems which neo-Marxists attacked at a moment well-calculated by them. The upcoming Olympic Games in Mexico City gave the left blackmail leverage over Mexican institutions. And callow masses of youth with Rousseauean notions provided the neo-Marxists with pawn-like shock troops to mount the assault.

49

Similarly, as soon as the draft was abolished in the U.S., violence on American campuses stopped, despite the fact that the Vietnam War was to rage on for more than two years. But not before American universities were "politicized," i.e., not before they adopted New Leftist orientations in curricula, and were coerced into taking political stands, invariably leftist. All were goals of the New Left in aiding the "inevitable" process of "History."

The counterculture mass thrust of the movement was content to achieve its less political, Rousseauean goal—doing away with required courses and academic authority in general, and the lowering of academic standards.

Clearly the forces that were loosed on the nation, and specifically on its colleges and universities, in the Vietnam War period predate the positivism of the modern social and behavioral sciences. Positivism did not do away with the Great Books, thus leaving a nihilistic vacuum filled by existentialism, as Bloom suggests. Rather the New Left's and the counterculture's thrusts are, sad to say, well rooted in Western civilization. The social and behavioral sciences stand justly accused by Bloom (and others before him) of specious claims to being value-free and having predictive power, i.e., of falsely and slavishly imitating the natural sciences because of their positivistic biases. But the idea of History in which nations, classes and civilizations give way to each other in dialectical process, and the ideal of natural youth corrupted by rigorous intellectual education, come from some of the very same Great Books of Western civilization—those of Hegel, Marx and Rousseau—the return to which as the curriculum of our colleges Bloom advances as his *only* solution to the crises of higher education.

Bloom's book is predicated on a single specious dualism. We have a choice only between nihilism (the view that human life and/or the universe is meaningless) and natural law. And we teach natural law by teaching the Great Books in colleges and universities.

Moreover, according to Bloom we can stave off nihilism only by teaching the Great Books to *only* a limited number of highly intellectual, correctly disposed students in a few small "serious" colleges. "Liberal education is what a small band of prestigious institutions are supposed to provide, in contrast to the big state schools." "The only solution is the one that is almost universally neglected: the good old Great Books approach," in which "classic texts" are read "as their authors wished them to be read," and "not treating them like historical products." "Only a few" people are capable of pursuing "truth," meaning truth about "Being," or a realm of ultimate reality beyond the ordinary world dealt with by the sciences and common sense. This is virtually the only type of truth that is worth pursuing in Bloom's view. Because Bloom believes in absolute, eternal truths, he has no use for "historicism," which he defines as "the view that all thought is essentially related to and cannot transcend its own time."

It should be noted that Bloom's insistence that relativism leads inevitably to nihilism is the very type of logical leap he criticizes in today's students in the opening paragraph of his book. Relative or contingent values are nevertheless values. If on the other hand he means that "relativism brings on nihilism" is merely a psychological truth, that lack of absolute truth brings on a mood of despair, he needs to verify this through empirical studies. But he presents us with none.

Bloom's ideal is the pre-Nazi "German university tradition, which...was the greatest expression of the publicly supported and approved version of the theoretical life. All were steeped in the general vision of humane education inspired by Kant and Goethe." "Men may live more truly and fully in reading Plato and Shakespeare than at any other time, because they are participating in essential being and are forgetting their accidental lives."

One does not have to go to the extreme of Bloom's rejections of everyday life, contemporary life, and the empirical sciences to appreciate there is great and indispensable value in reading Plato, Shakespeare and other classic authors. They set the eternal questions each generation and each person must deal with, and they set them with unexcelled intellectual depth, clarity, and in some cases esthetic power. But to seek in them one "unified view of nature and man's place in it" as Bloom does is fruitless. Bloom ignores the obvious objection that Plato, Shakespeare, Homer, Kant and other great thinkers and poets in Western history do not share one philosophy, be it natural law or other. Bloom speaks often as if they do, and at other times only as if they were all merely *searchers* for Being, also a dubious conclusion.

Bloom's answer to the quest for Being is natural law, determined by reason. But "reason" is used inconsistently by Bloom. Sometimes he seems to refer to rationalism in its strictest, technical sense, meaning the apprehension of truths about the world *a priori* to (before and independent of) empirical content, experience or evidence. This kind of rationalism is difficult to defend, to say the least, in the face of modern philosophy of knowledge. Indeed, Bloom makes no defense of it.

At other times, when Bloom uses "reason" he means something closer to what it meant to eighteenth century Enlightenment thinkers, a notion of reasoning as a generic, commonsense power of inquiry and accommodation, useful in reaching ideas of common good and social harmony. It is as in *Isaiah*'s invitation, "Come now, let us reason together." This sense of reason was that behind the U.S. Declaration of Independence and the U.S. Constitution. This meaning of reason was held to be a check against human impulses and passions, and a check against the closing off of reason by any passions, tyrannies or orthodoxies, including intellectual ones, presumably even those based on the absolute truths of natural law. This "reason" is distinctly *a posteriori*—it very much draws upon and makes its appeals to human observation and experience.

Bloom's confusing of the two meanings of reason is done in a way in which lack of faith in the first *(a priori)* meaning is made to entail the loss of faith in the second, Enlightenment sense. For example, he fuddles the two meanings of "reason" as he goes through extreme, almost Orwellian, intellectual contortions to convince the reader that our open society is closed:

> Openness used to be the virtue that permitted us to seek the good by using reason. It now means accepting everything and denying reason's power....Science's latest attempts to grasp the human situation— cultural relativism, historicism, the fact-value distinction—are the suicide of science. Culture, hence closedness, reigns supreme. Openness to closedness is what we teach.

We might add that in this last conclusion Bloom echoes a nonsensical criticism of open, democratic society made by Herbert Marcuse that was extremely popular with the New Left. It is the charge that openness is, in the famous phrase, "repressive tolerance." And no wonder at the echo. Both Marcuse and Bloom believe openness leads man to fritter away his essential nature instead of fulfilling it. Of course, the two thinkers have radically different ideas of what is essential human nature. To Marcuse, it is libidinal life energy. To Bloom it is the natural teleological "end" or purpose of the human species, which is man's capacity to reason, unique among living beings on earth.

Thus we come to Bloom's philosophy, natural law. He makes innumerable references to it and its corollaries in his book. For example, he counsels the "discovery of nature...what is accessible to all men as men through their common and distinctive faculty, reason." And he deplores our "loss of contact...with the natural order."

Natural law is a major philosophical tradition going back to Aristotle. In capsule form, it holds that purposes or laws of things are grounded in nature. Each species of life has its own distinguishing characteristic or nature, and the "good" for that species is the "free and unimpeded" development of that characteristic. For man, the distinguishing characteristic is his faculty of reason. Hence the good life is one in which reason is developed to its maximum. Natural law, as it were, is what reason discovers, and in turn natural law shows the moral supremacy of reason. All else is subordinated to the life of contemplation of absolute, unchanging truths known through *a priori* reasoning. Aristotle thought we could discover truths of *all* types this way, including truths in physics and other natural sciences. Contemporary natural law advocates like Bloom limit the claim to moral and sometimes to aesthetic truths.

In addition to the problems about rationalism already cited, there are a number of other very serious ones about natural law, none of which Bloom mentions. The tradition confuses the descriptive with the prescriptive. It confuses observations with "laws" or something to which we ought to conform or even be forced to conform. How are we to determine which of a species' unique characteristics is the critical one, forming the teleology to be followed and cultivated? For example, humanity is apparently the only species among mammals which deliberately kills its own kind, both in criminal homicide and in war. Why not subordinate reason and all else to the development of the qualities of warriors—strength, courage, loyalty, ferocity—in a military state? What about distinctly human love? Subordinate to reason? Why?

The most serious problem with natural law is that after over 2,000 years of its tradition there is no consensus among its own adherents on critical and basic moral questions. For example, is it moral to cultivate the competitive side of human nature, the cooperative side, or a balance? Specifically, what balance? Individual college grades or a collective one for the class? Private wealth or collective commonwealth? Is abstract art "natural"? What about emotional art as distinct from intellectual art? Are abstract and emotional art truly art? And what about *evolving* human nature? Evolving human conditions? Is it ever "natural" to "artificially" prolong life, and at what point, if any, may we pull the plug?

53

The point is that when we attempt to answer these and other moral and esthetic questions, and when we talk about human development, we find ourselves resorting to other principles and values instead of those of natural law.

Bloom is of no help regarding the vagueness of natural law. In fact, in the one instance in which he gives an example of a natural teleology, what he terms "the natural teleology of sex," his definition is so watered-down as to be empty, as is characteristic of the offerings of natural law theorists today. "I mean by teleology nothing but the evident, everyday observation and sense of purposiveness, *which may only be illusory,* but which guides human life, the kind everyone sees in the reproductive process." *[Emphasis added.]* And precisely *what* is it that "everyone sees"? One child for a married couple? A dozen? Is a "reasonable" use of birth control "natural?" Is sexual abstinence natural? Or oral sex?

The two strains in Western thought and history identified by Popper are fundamentally and irreconcilably incompatible with and hostile to an open, democratic society. One, the tradition of Hegel and Marx, would, and where in power, actually *does,* make society and individuals conform to pseudo-scientific "laws" of History. The other consists of Plato and others who would subordinate and shape society and individuals to conform to eternal, absolute, unchanging laws known by an elite few who have naturally superior capacity to reason, have most cultivated this capacity, and through it have grasped the absolute truths. The political side of the New Left (as distinct from the Rousseauean counterculture side) falls in the Hegel-Marx tradition. Bloom is in Plato's tradition.

Bloom makes his case by setting out sets of stark and false dualisms —an aristocracy based on natural law on one side versus equality, openness, history, "the useful," and the empirical social sciences on the other. He stacks the deck more by equating the latter side of the dualism with their most extreme distortions. So equality becomes egalitarianism, and openness becomes identical to Rousseauean and Hegelian neo-Marxist dogmas, *not* merely as the result of a deplorable but understandable and, it is to be hoped temporary, extreme lurch of attitudes in the context of particular time, the 1960s and 1970s. Social sciences are *inextricably* wed to dogmatic positivism in Bloom's view, and not merely in some of their early origins and in some lingering immature understandings of them. And when the social sciences are used and falsified for political or other corrupt ends, Bloom holds it is from their very *nature.*

As Bloom sees it, when pragmatic and empirical criteria are used to test and question the *a priori* notions gained in rational contemplation, they are *inherently* corrosive of truth and the human soul. When "democratic" movements denigrate excellence, tradition and reason (in its broader sense) they do so *inevitably* because democracy cannot in principle respect anything but the popular opinions of the moment. All of these identifications are a matter of logical, ontological, epistemological and psychological necessity for Bloom. There is only absolute, unchanging *a priori* truth on the one side, and error and nihilism on the other.

This farrago of dualisms is further confused by Bloom's constantly jumping back and forth between extreme and reasonable meanings of terms such as "equality" and "democracy," thus crisscrossing the fallacy of the undistributed middle with an agility that leads to startling conclusions that startle and dazzle us. They startle us because they defy the evidence of our experience, and they dazzle us because the logical sleight of hand is so deft we can't immediately see why. So we get such passages as:

..."The aspiration to be number one and gain great fame is both natural in man and, properly trained, one of the soul's great strengths. Democracy in itself is hostile to such spiritness and prevents its fulfillment."

..."But openness, nevertheless, eventually won out over natural rights, partly through a theoretical critique, partly because of a rebellion against nature's last constraints."

..."A very great narrowness is not incompatible with the health of an individual or a people, whereas with great openness it is hard to avoid decomposition."

...A "small number" of people will want to live a contemplative life as opposed to the great masses who "will be content with what our present considers relevant" and "others [who] will have a spirit of enthusiasm that subsides as family and ambition provide them with other objects of interest....It is for these [the small number]...especially that liberal education exists. They become models for the noblest human faculties and hence are benefactors to all of us, more for what they are than for what they do."

..."It was not necessarily the best of times in America when Catholics and Protestants were suspicious of and hated one another; but at least they were taking their beliefs seriously."

..."The professors of humanities...are essentially involved with interpreting and transmitting old books, preserving what we call tradition, in a democratic order where tradition is not privileged. They are partisans of the leisured and beautiful in a place where evident utility is the only passport. Their realm is the always and the contemplative, in a setting that demands only the here and now and the active. The justice in which they [as creatures of our time] believe is egalitarian, and they are the agents of the rare, the refined and the superior. By definition they are out of it, and their democratic inclinations and guilt push them to be with it."

Bloom refuses to consider that one may have ambitions and value family and still cultivate one's mind, or that the cultivation of the rules and habits of scientific thinking and of all forms of intelligence and esthetic sensibilities can constitute education and the development of human potential, even "natural" potential if you will. And where are his examples of societies of "healthy narrowness"? Lebanon? Iran? Northern Ireland, where Catholics and Protestants are still "taking their beliefs seriously"?

In the end, then, what Bloom is arguing for is bondage of the American mind to an orthodoxy of undefinable absolute truths apprehended by an alleged intellectual elite who have no consensus among themselves, the subordination of American education, values and society to these wills o' the wisps, and the destruction of American democracy appropriate to rule by a fictitious aristocracy of superior beings "who are models for the use of the noblest human faculties and hence are benefactors to all of us, more for what they are than for what they do."

Pressures on colleges to make the education they offer conform to an orthodoxy, to a special illumination, or to urgent needs are not limited to Bloom's arguments. Nor are all of them new. In the 1950s, colleges, because of their ideal ethic of academic freedom to seek and teach the truth independent of all biases, were being labelled as neglectful, if not subversive, in not teaching patriotic values needed for national survival against the Soviet Union's threat. Cries of other urgencies are heard today in calls for colleges to teach "civic values" that will fortify the nation in its struggle with the USSR.

For example, the 1985 report of the Carnegie Foundation for the Advancement of Teaching, known as the "Newman Report," approvingly cites pressures for economic growth, increasing international and technological competition, a need for civic-minded Americans, the problem of peace and nuclear arms, needs to control genetic engineering, achieving "economic stability without stagnation, inflation, or poverty," "reduction of crime, drugs, and violence," and "effective cooperation among increasingly interconnected nations." It goes on to urge "creation of links between business and the university and business and the schools." It continues, "All young men and women should be encouraged to serve the country." In the last regard, the Newman Report cites examples running from the Civilian Conservation Corps of the 1930s to the Peace Corps and the Teacher Corps.

In the 1960s and 1970s, the demand was that college education be made "relevant"—meaning it should serve liberal and leftist reform agendas of that period. In the 1980s, the great prevailing pressure became to make higher education relevant, that is servile, to a quite different agenda—the vocational and careerist interests of students and the domestic and international interests of the American economy. And colleges and universities are giving in to the pressures of careerism and international economic competitiveness with an alacrity almost as great as that they displayed in their cave-in to the New Left and counterculture a scant twenty or twenty-five years ago.

A 1986 study of colleges and universities by the American Council on Education showed that while colleges expected to keep the numbers of their faculty unchanged in most disciplines over the next five years, 59 percent of them expected to hire more teachers of computer science and 41 percent expected to hire more faculty to teach business courses. In light of the neglect of the humanities, social sciences and natural sciences in higher education today, the decision not to increase faculty and courses in them is indefensible.

While the intent to hire computer and business teachers is laudatory, we must be clear that it will be done at the expense of the humanities, social sciences and natural sciences, both in terms of numbers of faculty in each area, and in how they are rewarded. It adds up to a further weakening of colleges. As one college president put it, "I hear 'supply and demand' until it makes me sick. My concern is how to maintain a sense of community in the face of this dysfunction."

Giving in to the trends of the day in fact means giving in to *irrelevance*. A narrowly based education, be it towards the ends of social reform, individual careers or national economic needs, becomes obsolete with the next trend or need. As the longshoreman-philosopher Eric Hoffer put it, "In a time of drastic change it is the learners who inherit the future. The learned usually find themselves equipped to live in a world that no longer exists."

Aggravating the probable further decline in humanities education is the prediction that, for the first time in two decades, there will be a *shortage*

57

instead of a surplus of people with PhDs in the humanities and social sciences vis-á-vis the number of college teaching positions opening in these areas. This is according to a thorough study, *Prospects for Faculty in the Arts and Sciences: Demand and Supply 1987-2012*. (Princeton University Press, 1989.) The prediction is that from 1997-2002 there will be 0.8 eligible people for each faculty opening in *all* areas, opposed to 1.6 potential candidates in 1992. The report attributes this situation to a "flight from the liberal arts and sciences" in the 1970s and 1980s. (The first decade, we might note, was a period of politically and socially "relevant" education, and the second a time of vocationally "relevant" education.) Restoring balance between qualified potential candidates in the sciences requires a 64 percent increase in the annual number of PhDs being earned in scientific fields. Achieving a balance in the social sciences and humanities would require a 92 percent increase in the PhDs earned annually in those areas. There are no signs that any of these increases are likely to occur.

Many of the counterculture graduates of the late 1960s and the 1970s were unable to meet the challenges of the 1980s, except by recourse to the yuppie and other stunted, privatistic modes of living. In the phrase of one commentator, they've become "born again bourgeoisie"—with a vengeance. Middle-aged Babbitts are just as "irrelevant" to critical concerns as are middle-aged flower children—unless, of course, in their middle age they finally educate themselves, as Mario Savio did in the 1980s. And the strictly careerist oriented students of today are similarly dooming their future, and the nation's.

Surveys of student interests, abetted by pressures from corporate America, and students' actual enrollment in courses reflect a strong bias toward career, professional or vocational education, and away from "impractical" courses as well as from the ideal of a liberal education itself. That ideal needs to be examined in the light of the claims and realities of our time.

4.

Liberal Education: Purposes and Curricula

I USE the word "liberal" in *liberal education* in the traditional meaning
that distinguishes liberal education from education that is "servile." Servile
education serves any interests or goals other than the intrinsic goals of
education itself. And this is regardless of how worthy, pressing or noble
the extrinsic goals.

Traditionally, the goals of liberal education have been the cultivation
of the mind and character of the individual student. Colleges attempted
to achieve these liberal education goals even after vocational and other
aims were added to the purposes of a college education, starting in the
nineteenth century. At liberal arts colleges, the vocational, career and
professional goals *supplemented* the central liberal goals. They did not do
away with them. That is, until the last twenty-five years.

The counterculturists of the late 1960s and the 1970s left a vacuum
in place of the liberal arts core of college education they swept from American campuses, and the New Left and commercialist influences attempted
and still attempt to fill the great emptiness. The New Left attempts to
do so with its ideologically political goals, and the latter with its practical
and patriotic goals. The New Left should not be discounted. Its efforts
are far from spent, and many of its advocates are today strategically placed
in the administrations and faculties of colleges. They include individuals
who were themselves New Left student activists in the Vietnam War period.
One former student activist, now a professor of English at Middlebury College, was forthright about it in 1989. "After the Vietnam War," he wrote,

"a lot of us didn't just crawl back into academic positions...Now we have tenure, and the hard work of reshaping the universities has begun in earnest."

Nevertheless, it is clear today that personal careerist and corporate business goals have triumphed at least as much as the New Left in filling higher education's great gap of purpose created by the flower children. One of the great ironies in higher education is that the hippies and New Leftists of the Johnson-Nixon years made colleges safe for business-student yuppie-university alliances in the Reagan-Bush years. College education has become servile to narrowly defined, short-sighted goals of corporate America, and the perceived career and job interests of intellectually callow students. The trend is underway with great momentum. The momentum is, as the phrase goes, "made possible by" two of the innumerable false dualisms that seem always to plague thinking about education. One is "the useful versus the useless." And the other is "process versus content."

The dichotomy between the useful and the useless is nurtured by "high-minded" philosophers like Allan Bloom who despise "pragmatism" and see the goal of education as growth toward a *fixed* aim defined by human nature. The inner life of contemplation is touted as all important. As Bloom puts it, a man is worthy not so much for what he does but for what he is.

The attitude, if not the argument, reminds one of Emerson's idea of the great man, and Melville's response to it. Emerson saw the great man as one who creates a moral climate through his abstract instruction of others, but who personally remains aloof from the moral affairs of men. Melville has one of the characters in *The Confidence-Man* say of the Emersonian great man that it is easy for him to keep a cool head because of the ice in his heart. In contrast to Emerson's and Bloom's concepts the liberal educational ideal sees the inner life of a person and his practical life as a well-integrated whole, and not as separate or antagonistic functions.

At the other extreme from contemplativists is the view exemplified by today's emphasis on careerism. When it dominates, as it did increasingly on American campuses in the late 1980s, education fosters the development of free-floating specialized skills and knowledge at the neglect of any larger meanings into which they should be rooted or to which they can be related. Making education into merely business or professional training, or a tagged-on adjunct of such training, produces graduates who are one-dimensional ignoramuses. They make up much of the ranks of the graduates of the past two-and-a-half decades.

The solution may lie in relating and integrating some liberal education with specialized training and knowledge that may have market value. But it surely should not lie in abandoning the goals of the cultivation of the mind and character of the individual or subordinating them to market needs. The methods, perspectives and values of the humanities, the social sciences and the natural sciences need to be the dominant context in which special skills and knowledge are learned and employed. There is all the difference in the world between a career education and a thorough liberal education with a specialization in a marketable area or discipline of studies. It is the difference between skills integrated into an examined life and skills which purport to be ends in themselves.

In the final analysis, the issue is drawn between those who believe that well educated people will be up to the challenges of the day and the unforeseeable ones of the future, and those who fear those challenges and would shackle and narrow human potential. The Babbitts of today's big business, who purport to revere "free" market forces in the economic sphere, have no faith in liberally educating people. That is, they have no faith in the free mind, disciplined only by the criteria of the mind.

The word "purport" is used here because many of the current Babbitts see the economy as something to be manipulated in endless paper games of acquisitions and mergers. The junk bond market was only $1 billion in 1981, but by 1988 it had grown to $180 billion. Hostile takeovers, and the exploitive running of acquired companies into the ground—because the *acquired* company is obliged to pay off on the high-yield junk bonds used in the takeover—do not produce goods. Every great capitalist theorist since Adam Smith wrote his *Wealth of Nations* in 1776 has understood that the heart of capitalism lies in its ability to create wealth by producing consumable goods. *All* wealth depends ultimately on production of consumable goods. Economic value is created when labor is added to raw materials to produce goods, goods whose value is greater than that of the simple sum of the unrelated labor and raw materials. That nation is wealthy which can produce goods itself or can control the production of goods by other nations. The pursuit of economic wealth on any other criteria is the building of a house of cards.

Acquisitions capitalism flies in the face of Smith's demonstration that money as such is not wealth. A nation whose economic system is based on merely playing with the money it holds, merely moving it from company to company or from person to person, is not creating wealth. Understood by these basic criteria of true capitalism, acquisitions capitalism is dangerously weakening the economic viability and power of the United States. Worse, the takeover mania has forced American companies deeper into their bad habit of paying attention to short-term profits at the expense of long-term research and development and capital investment. This at a time when the latter are absolutely essential in the economic competition against Europe, Japan and other Pacific Rim countries.

In the 1980s the illusion of growing wealth was kept up by the federal government's subsidations of consumer debt. Indeed, some 80 percent of the Gross National Product is accounted for by consumer spending, bringing to mind Errol Flynn's remark that "my net income can't keep pace with my gross habits." The federal government subsidized consumer spending through its deficit spending, and through incentives to foreign investors in U.S. government securities to help service the national debt without raising taxes. The government thus encouraged the illusion that the U.S. can transform itself into a "service economy" and still have a first-rate competitive economy. A service economy that depends on the manufactures of other nations is an economic colony, and will not long enjoy economic wealth or power.

Acquisitions capitalism is a perversion and subversion of capitalism. It gives profits without production. Its claim to lead to more efficient production is belied by the 1980s' low manufacturing productivity. In the end, acquisitions capitalism is nothing but economic masturbation. If it is continued, the nation will continue to lose in economic competition with other, more productive nations.

The solution to America's crisis of international economic competition lies in political reform of the economy, putting it back into productive modes rather than letting more and more of it go into merely manipulative modes. The solution does *not* lie in higher education abandoning its proper purpose and goals in favor of those set by business, least of all by business which is dominated by pseudo-capitalist, short-sighted, manipulative, nonproductive greed.

A career education lacking the greater context of a liberal education and its goals fossilizes the graduate as soon as his narrow skills and knowledge become dated, as they surely will. And, of course, to the extent the *educated* citizenry is made up of narrowly trained ignoramuses, the civic as well as economic needs of a complex democratic republic will suffer grievously. For one of the greatest *useful* characteristics, if you will, of a liberally educated person is his ability to participate more widely and deeply in the polity and culture of his lifetime, and possibly to contribute to them.

In short, the opposite of a liberal education is not practical education but training that is useless in terms of the wider and deeper aspects of the individual and of his culture and polity. The poverty of a narrowly trained mind and character diminishes itself first, and every thing and every one else in addition.

In the late 1980s, there was a crescendo of cries to return education to "content" instead of "process," the latter of course meaning teaching the processes of thinking. Chief among the fallacies underlying this demand is the illusion that colleges since the counterculture debacle have in fact been teaching students to think. They have not. More important, the dualism between learning to think and learning content is a nonsensical one on its face. Thinking without thinking *about something*? Learning content without *thinking* about it?

Yet we leaned toward the latter inanity in the 1950s. The complaint was that the emphasis upon required courses and programs of study had grown so formalistic that colleges lost sight of the educational purposes the requirements were to serve, or did not adequately communicate them to students. Consequently, the required studies were perceived by students as burdensomely huge piles of pointless "Mickey Mouse" items to memorize. It was an exhausting preoccupation with poorly understood or appreciated, and hence "dead," information. For example, often the emphasis was not on learning to appreciate, through reading assigned plays by Shakespeare, the beauty and value of poetry as an art expressing meanings of life and Shakespeare's insights about the human condition. Instead it was on having to memorize deadly pedantic knowledge *about* Shakespeare's plays.

And there is more than just a germ of justification in the complaint that higher education in the 1950s had become too "bookish" in the sense that students were not guided, not *educated*, to see how what they studied in *Western Civilization*, or in *Survey of Music*, or in *Physical Science for Liberal Arts Students*, had meaning and value for them.

But discontent with the 1950s' formalism and pedantry did not, in fact, lead to a reform of teaching students the processes of thinking. Instead, it led to the nihilism of the counterculture and the agitation-propaganda and political indoctrination of the New Left. The cries being raised today against "process oriented education" are raised against a straw man.

The same straw man has come under assault, for example, in E.D. Hirsch's best-selling book, *Cultural Literacy*. The book argues that every student should know a long list of facts, which he can then place in insightful contexts. But Hirsch then negates the emphasis on insightful contexts and presents a 5,000 item list of facts, as one reviewer termed it, running from A ("act of God") to Z (*"Zeitgeist"*), including "White Christmas" ("song") under W. That this silliness is taken seriously should be as shocking as the fact that Reich's counterculture paean to natural process, *The Greening of America* was taken seriously in the early 1970s.

Hirsch's approach of using recognized, memorized, facts or information as a test of learning, is a pendulum swing away from Reich's breathless reliance on a thin neo-Rousseauean anti-intellectual natural process. That both books received serious attention, each in its respective decade, is evidence that many still think about education in the false context of the "facts vs. process" dualism. As Dewey noted in 1904, the educational pendulum swings endlessly between poles of this sterile dualism as it does between other dualisms. The "content" versus "thinking" educational fallacy in which Hirsch traps himself is as old as memory. But it was well answered as early as the sixth century B.C. The *Analects* report that Confucius said, "To learn without thinking is in vain. To think without learning is dangerous."

We do need to teach college students to *think*. We need to teach them to think by teaching *all* students to think in the models, habits and processes of the various disciplines, to experience the world in the ways of the different arts, and through these thrusts to develop students' characters. "Character" here refers to the commonsense, ordinary meanings of the word found in the dictionary. Webster defines "character" as "The aggregate of distinctive qualities belonging to an individual; the stamp of individuality impressed by nature, education, and habit; the estimate put on a person; moral vigor or firmness as acquired through discipline."

These liberal goals and means of education obviously are not in any way at odds with students' learning the content of the disciplines of the humanities, the social sciences and the natural sciences. On the contrary. We could see them at odds only if we define "content" to mean merely "facts," practical skills demanded by the marketplace, or patriotic doctrines without the context of a liberal education. The person who has a liberal education can place them, challenge them, enlarge them, forever rethink them in the light of experience and further education, and thus actively shape them and give them meanings instead of passively receiving them as unchanging, sacred verities.

In the end, when we examine the cries for a return to a "content oriented" education we find at their heart commitments to making higher education servile to economic and national interests or patriotic goals perceived precisely according to orthodoxies of the time, as doctrinaire in their way as is the New Left's model of education. The difference between *educating* students about an idea, and *indoctrinating* students with an idea, is that in education the students are required to understand what they are taught, and are also taught conflicting ideas and competing ideas. In indoctrination, students are required to believe what they are being taught and become intellectually or morally committed to it over any and all other ideas.

Increasing numbers of colleges are reinstituting required courses. In March of 1986, the American Council on Education issued a report of a survey conducted over eighteen months. It showed that 28 percent of colleges had already reintroduced required courses, and another 27 percent indicated they were planning to do so. Eighty percent of these schools said they were instituting general education requirements, but with most of the courses aimed at students attaining only the college equivalent of the "Three Rs"— writing, mathematics, communications and reasoning. These reforms fall far short of the need.

In the opinion of every serious study since the mid-1980s, the general education requirements, where they exist at all, are too few, do not form a comprehensive or even coherent curriculum core, and their sum educational effect is poor. To cite one typical example, a 1985 report of the Association of American Colleges was as scathing in its assessment of 1980s' reforms as it was of what it terms the "supermarket" curricula inherited from the Vietnam War period:

> The curriculum has given way to a marketplace philosophy: it is a supermarket where students are shoppers and professors are merchants of learning. Fads and fashions, the demands of popularity and success, enter where wisdom and experience should prevail....The marketplace philosophy refuses to establish common expectations and norms. Another victim of this philosophy is the general education

of the American college graduate, the institutional requirements outside the major. They lack a rationale and cohesion, or even worse, are almost lacking altogether. Electives are being used to fatten majors and diminish breadth. It is as if no one cared, so long as the store stays open.

One of the saddest ironies about the narrow training today's students receive instead of a coherent and comprehensive grounding in life-long education is evident in a comment of a member of the eighteen-member Advisory Commission of the Office of Technology Assessment of the U.S. Congress. Said Dr. Michael Hooker, president of the University of Maryland at Baltimore:

> Suppose we take a student and train him in the latest technology of the day, give him a real state of the art knowledge so he is at the cutting edge of technology. Within five years all of those skills are going to be obsolete and all of the knowledge he has will be obsolete.
> ...The challenge [is] to educate students in such a way that they can deal with it [the future] personally, psychologically, and in terms of the skills they bring to the jobs they have. I say the liberal arts education is the best education for that.

To give students narrow career training and an inadequate, noncomprehensive general education shortchanges them and the culture and polity in which they live. Thus it cheats all of us, for it limits the graduates' capacities to participate in and contribute to the social, cultural and civic affairs of their lifetimes, as well as limiting their capacities to think about questions of morality, love and mortality each individual must meet in his personal life.

To build on what has been said, the foremost overall aim of higher education should be to teach *all* students to think according to the models of the humanities, the social sciences and the natural sciences, to appreciate the world through the arts, and especially to develop in students the disposition to continue to advance these capacities throughout their lives.

Colleges have the obligation and the authority that come from the wisdom and experience of learning to require students to study what the colleges deem is needed to be an educated person and citizen. It is time they exercised that authority again. All of the reports of special commissions and committees of the mid and late 1980s emphasized the point in differing ways.

Among the most vigorous of the recommendations are those found in the National Endowment for the Humanities' 1984 report, *To Reclaim A Legacy.* The NEH Report focused on recommendations regarding a general education all students should receive. Broadly, the report recommends that: 1) the humanities be given a central place in the required core curriculum; 2) that each college, via its required general education, define what knowledge is essential for an educated person; and 3) the general humanities education be an integrated one.

Specifically, the NEH Report recommends meeting these goals through the following programs of courses:

A. An understanding of the origin and development of Western civilization, and the chronology of its development from its roots in the ancient world to the present. This program should stress major developments in society, art, religion, literature and politics.

B. The careful study of masterworks of American, English and European literature.

C. Study of the most important issues and ideas in the history of philosophy.

D. Study of a foreign language with emphasis of such study as an avenue into another culture.

E. Study of the history of science and technology.

F. A study of the history, literature, religion and philosophy of at least one non-Western culture or civilization.

The strengths of the NEH's recommended required core curriculum are in its rationale and its comprehensiveness. It aims at turning out graduates who have a basic grounding in their own American culture and Western civilization, coupled with antidotes to American and Western parochialisms which may be had in some knowledge of non-American and non-Western cultures, a basic understanding of the content of the natural sciences, and a background in the record of great thoughts about the perennial questions of what it means to be a human being.

The very serious weakness of the NEH core curriculum lies in its seeming neglect of giving students an understanding of the content and methods of the social sciences.

In 1985, the Carnegie Foundation for the Advancement of Teaching issued a report on "higher education policy," which has come to be known as the Newman Report, after Frank Newman, the chairman of the commission that produced the report. The Newman Report comes down squarely on the side of the useful in setting a "national policy" for higher education and having colleges and students conform to that policy.

The policy is stated in terms of two goals higher education should serve. One is the economy of the U.S. (both in its domestic and international aspects), done by turning students into what the report terms "entrepreneurs." The other goal is "committed citizenship," to be achieved by colleges' teaching "civic skills."

The Newman Report proclaims, "It is essential that the purpose of a liberal education be transformed so that it provides not only a broad base of knowledge and the requisite intellectual skills, but that it develops an entrepreneurial spirit and a sense of civic responsibility, subjects that are seldom discussed on campus."

By way of justifying its proposed national educational policy, the Newman Report cites the urgency of the international competitive economic needs of the United States—"the jolt of growing competition, most notably from Japan"—and a list of domestic economic goals to be served by higher education: "accelerate economic growth and job formation"; "attract advanced technology industry"; "invest in the research universities in order to improve the research base and the numbers of technically trained graduates"; and "create links between business and the universities and the schools." Colleges and universities are to be fully mobilized in the national economic effort: "We believe that the United States is gearing up for an economic renewal. Education at all levels is expected to play a major role."

To justify reshaping and subordinating higher education to civic as well as economic goals, the Newman Report cites a seemingly random list of urgent "societal issues of enormous complexity and seriousness—issues such as, how to accelerate the integration of growing and diverse minorities, how to control the continuing proliferation of nuclear arms, and how to reduce the dangers of toxic wastes."

The Newman Report's caution that "care and restraint are required to insure that one does not slip across the line from values to ideology" in setting and implementing its national higher education policy is in direct self-contradiction to the report's goal. Its "useful," issues and needs-oriented education, however urgent or worthy these may be, is the very antithesis of a liberal education. It sets up needs and goals of our time, as seen of course by the report's authors, as primary educational goals, rather than the liberal goals of cultivating the mind of the student—his disciplined thinking skills and his character disposition to continue to learn.

If the history of the last three decades has demonstrated anything, it has shown that the "paramount" needs of society and the economy change radically, both in fact and in how they are popularly perceived. Yesterday's "with it" graduate is left with a narrow, outdated education, and lacks the discipline skills to advance his education to keep up with changes. "Yippies" have been replaced by "yuppies" over twenty years, but there is no notable intellectual or moral growth perceptible in the change.

For all of its hard-headed business and civic focus, the curricular formula of the Newman Report is trendy and doctrinaire. It would continue the whipsawing of higher education between sets of extrinsic goals. Yesterday, counterculture and New Left revolution. Today, business needs and social reform. In the words of Yogi Berra, "It's *deja vu* all over again."

It's time for higher education to liberate itself by vigorously and victoriously asserting again that it is not the servant of political, economic, religious, moral or social movements or trends.

In sharp contrast, another report issued in 1985, by the National Institute of Education (NIE), stressed that "The college curriculum has become excessively vocational in its orientation, and the bachelor's degree has lost its potential to foster the shared values and knowledge that bind us together as a society." The NIE Report goes on to recommend that "All bachelor's degree recipients should have at least two full years of liberal education." The NIE's reason for making this recommendation is succinctly put: "We thus conclude that the best preparation for the future is not narrow training for a specific job, but rather an education that will enable students to adapt to a changing world."

Given the diversity of disciplines to be learned and the wealth of knowledge in a liberal education, the requirement that two years be devoted to it is not excessive. But the NIE is incorrect in asserting that this will require that for most students the time devoted to earning a bachelor's degree be in increased from four to five years. Assuming that a bachelor's degree requires a minimum of about 120 credits, usual in American colleges, this would mean 60 credits would be devoted to a general liberal arts education. Most colleges require about 30 credits for a major, which would leave 30 credits open for elective courses—ten courses at the usual allocation of three credits per course. This does not seem burdensomely restrictive. The scheme is premised on full-time students taking 15 credits a semester, or five 3-credit courses. Twelve to fifteen credits is the usual traditional full-time course load.

Students wishing to take more electives could take an additional three-credit course a semester for as many semesters they elect to do so, for a maximum potential of an additional 24 credits, or eight courses, thus raising the total maximum number of electives to 18 courses or 54 credits. And a student could take as many of these extra electives as he wishes in his area of major study.

Of course this would require that the student taking 18 credits in a given semester work more than if he were taking 15. (The extra electives could be taken in summer school, but this would not be attractive to some students who need summer employment to earn money or who want to travel.) But it is reasonable to assume that a student who is motivated to take extra electives would have the will to work a bit harder. There is certainly no reason to assume that he will do worse in terms of grades for the extra work, and thus be penalized when applying for a job or to a graduate school.

Indeed, undergraduate colleges could "flag" the transcripts of its graduates who voluntarily pursued extra education beyond what the institution required. Precedent for this exists. Some colleges flag grades of "A" on transcripts received during the Vietnam era to indicate whether all students in the course got an "A" or whether grades were distributed in the course. Employers and graduate schools would no doubt be inclined to favor hard-working students in their selections of employees or graduate students, especially during the present time when there are widespread complaints that many college students have a lackadaisical attitude toward study and work. Colleges, foundations and governments might provide tuition assistance to cover the cost of the extra education.

We must also consider that 5 million of the 12 million American undergraduates are part-time students, with jobs or other responsibilities beyond their studies. The largest increase in the student population is found in these usually older, "nontraditional" students, as they have come to be known. They, of course, take more than four years to complete their undergraduate education, and might not elect to prolong the time further by taking electives beyond the number required. But there is reason to believe that these students, in their maturity, place a higher value on a general, liberal education than do the seventeen to twenty-two year-old full-time students—ask any instructor who has taught both groups in recent years.

In addition, the NIE Report makes the recommendation that the required program of studies should stress the "development [in students] of the capacities of analysis, problem solving, communication, and synthesis." Although the report does not specify how this is to be accomplished, a liberal education that teaches students to think in the discipline models of the social sciences, natural sciences and the humanities would well serve this goal.

Happily, the NIE Report goes on to recommend that "students and faculty integrate knowledge from various disciplines." This is addressed to the problem that, as the NIE Report puts it, echoing complaints of the 1950s and 1960s, "What happens too often when liberal education requirements are increased is fragmentation" of knowledge the student receives, and "the task of integrating knowledge, though central to liberal education, is frequently ignored in favor of analysis." The result is that the student's ability to integrate what he has learned in the various disciplines into coherent abilities to understand the world remains undeveloped.

To correct this, the NIE Report recommends, first, closer collaboration among faculty from different departments. Indeed, there is at present very little *intellectual* intercourse between faculty from different departments, their limited interaction being largely confined to mundane and routine practical matters such as scheduling of courses. Requiring departments to collaborate in designing a coherent program of general education and giving faculty incentives to teach the courses in the program might impel college instructors to integrate their areas of knowledge with wider views of the world. It is an effort which many teachers have not made since their own undergraduate days, and many, especially those who were undergraduates since the mid-1960s, have never attempted at all.

In the 1980s it emerged that one of the practical problems in offering required courses, and especially multidisciplinary courses, is the scarcity of faculty on campuses well-educated enough to teach them. This is particularly true of younger faculty who received their undergraduate education since the mid-1960s. Thus, a dean at the college where I teach told me, in response to an article I wrote urging more coherent programs of study, that some administrators at the college felt some relief at the abandonment of required courses in the 1970s. There were increasing problems in staffing some of the courses. (The college has since reintroduced required studies, albeit in reduced and less coherent modes.)

A 1985 report of the American Association of Colleges (AAC) not only protests that "As for what passes as college curriculum, almost anything goes," but also applies this criticism to the curricula of concentrations of study, the "majors," as well as to the students' general education. "Indeed," says the AAC Report, "the major in most colleges is little more than a gathering of courses taken in one department, lacking structure and depth, as is often the case in the humanities and social sciences, or emphasizing content to the neglect of the essential style of inquiry on which the content is based, as is too frequently true in the natural and physical sciences."

As a remedy, the AAC Report offers nine goals for any curricula, and for *all* students, to meet the requirements of a bachelor's degree, a degree which the AAC Report says has become quite literally "meaningless." In stating some of the goals, the AAC Report doesn't develop the purpose of education it seems to suggest, the goal of giving students an understanding of modes of thinking in the social sciences, natural sciences and the humanities when it speaks of the "essential style of inquiry" underlying a discipline. In considering mathematics, history and ethics, it leans in some regards to another "useful" rather than liberal scheme of education, although on a much higher order of sophistication and aims than the Newman Report's utilitarian goals of entrepreneurial values and civic consciousness. The temptation today to win people to the cause of higher education by convincing them of its practical uses seems irresistible. Yet the goals urged in the AAC Report are, on balance, well put and deserve attention:

1. Mathematics. "Students should encounter concepts that permit a sophisticated response to arguments and positions which depend on numbers and statistics."

2. History. "The more refined our historical understanding, the better prepared we are to recognize complexity, ambiguity, and uncertainty as intractable conditions of human society."

3. Literacy. "A bachelor's degree should mean that its holders can read, write, and speak at levels of distinction and have been given many opportunities to learn how. It also should mean that many of them do so with style."

4. Science. The report recommends that students understand scientific method, and the "human, social, and political implications of scientific research."

5. Values or ethics. Students should learn to "make real choices, as-

sume responsibility for their decisions, be comfortable with their own behavior, and know why."

6. Art. "Without a knowledge of the language of the fine arts, we see less and hear less," and "Without some experience in the performing arts we are denied the knowledge of disciplined creativity and its meaning as a bulwark of freedom and an instrument of social cohesion."

7. Multicultural understanding. "Colleges must create a curriculum in which the insights and understandings, the lives and aspirations of the distant and foreign, the different and neglected, are more widely comprehended by their graduates."

8. Methods of understanding and appreciation. "To reason well, to recognize when reason and evidence are not enough, to discover the legitimacy of intuition, to subject inert data to the probing analysis of the mind— these are the primary experiences required of the undergraduate course of study."

9. Cohesive, in-depth knowledge and insight. "Depth requires sequential learning, building on blocks of knowledge that lead to more sophisticated understanding and encourage leaps of the imagination and efforts at synthesis."

The last point of stressing sequential learning raises one of the current controversies as many colleges attempt to form or reform required curricula. It is that of strict "core" requirements versus "distribution" requirements. Core requirements, at their most rigorous, provide a program of exactly the same courses for all students, and the courses are taken in precisely the same sequence by all students.

Proponents of core requirements cite its cohesive, in-depth potential. Also, requiring a student to study a given discipline or course may, and often does, create an interest in him that would otherwise lie unknown, perhaps throughout his life, if he were allowed to choose in ignorance from among requirements. He would thereby neglect something that is in his interest to know, and perhaps also in the interests of his culture and society that he understand or appreciate.

Critics of this scheme cite its inflexibility as a Procrustean bed which all students are forced to fit regardless of their individual differences in abilities and interests. But they are obligated to argue reasonably how students are qualified by knowledge to choose their courses of general education, since such ability presupposes that the student is already educated at the college level. Instead, the critics of required general education usual-

73

ly resort to an argument of "democratic free choice," often accompanied by the charge that requirements are "elitist."

As one man wrote in response to a 1987 magazine article of mine on higher education, it is "tyranny" for a college to require its students to take courses. Of course, the premise is flawed. The model of democracy is inappropriate where the authority of learning is involved. But it is precisely this travesty of misapplied democracy that was forced on colleges by the Rousseauean counterculture assault which peaked in the late 1960s and early 1970s, and which left us with the "supermarket" model of college curricula justly being criticized today.

Some critics of core requirements still favor requirements, but in the distribution curriculum model. In this attempt at compromise, students are given a choice, but only from among alternative requirements set by the college. It is widely dubbed "the Chinese restaurant menu" approach. For example, Harvard, after doing away with required courses in the 1960s and 1970s, implemented a core curriculum of about 150 courses in six broad areas. Students must select 25 percent of their undergraduate studies from these.

Distribution-requirements schemes can meet the needs of a liberal general education *provided* that faculty approve chosen combinations of courses of study possible in the offerings to students so that the choices result in the comprehensive, in-depth education that I have stressed. Otherwise it can, and in fact often does, result in individual students amassing required credits in an incoherent, incomplete or even bizarre collection of courses. In other words, this latter type of unsupervised required "distribution" education is just another form of supermarket education.

Still another influential report on higher education was released in 1986. It came from the Carnegie Foundation for the Advancement of Teaching, and has come to be known as the "Boyer Report," after the Foundation's president, Ernest L. Boyer. It too is extremely critical of the whole enterprise of higher education. "Driven by careerism," the Boyer Report says, "and overshadowed by graduate and professional education, many of the nation's colleges and universities are more successful in credentialing than in providing a quality education for their students. It is not that the failure of the undergraduate college is so large but that the expectations are so small."

The aim of the Boyer Report is to raise those expectations, stressing an "integrated core" in the form of requirements set up on a premise of seven interdisciplinary areas of studies, each set around a theme. The thematic structure is already in use in a number of colleges. The Boyer Report recommends the following version of it:

1. Language [English language skills]: The Crucial Connection.
2. Art: The Esthetic Experience.
3. Heritage: The Living Past.
4. Institutions: The Social Web.
5. Nature: The Ecology of the Planet.
6. Work: The Value of Vocation.
7. Identity: The Search for Meaning.

The Boyer Report stresses that its recommended curriculum for general education "is not something to 'get out of the way,' but should extend vertically from freshman to senior year. In a properly designed baccalaureate program, general education and specialized education will be joined."

The Boyer Report's attempt to integrate required programs of study into cohesive wholes is laudable. The courses making up the programs in each theme would have to be carefully selected with regard to the other courses and the whole program. Haphazard selection by students from among a distribution of offered courses won't do. The adoption of a thematic approach by a college does not automatically meet its obligation to offer a comprehensive set of required courses but merely *highlights* this necessity by focusing on the need to give definition to the whole.

But is anything achieved by calling history "The Living Past" instead of "history"? And does studying The Ecology of the Planet give the student an understanding of the natural sciences' disciplines that will serve him throughout life? Or does it give him just another content course? If the latter, why not another theme in science, e.g., "The Expanding Universe" or "The Chemistry of Life?" Instead of "Institutions: The Social Web," why not "People, Power and Politics"? In other words the dangers of the thematic approach are that it invites trendy content-oriented, "headlines" courses at the expense of cultivating students' abilities to think and appreciate the world in terms of the major learned disciplines. In addition, the themes chosen are extremely vague, as in "Identity: The Search for Meaning," and can easily become a catch-all for a distribution of courses that are in fact connected poorly, if at all.

Objections to the very idea that there should be required general education fall into two types, those which object in principle, and those which raise practical obstacles.

The only "principled" objection, apart from the argument from misplaced democracy, is the one that says it is impossible to say which course of general study is best for students. This begs the question of whether a college can say students, society and culture would benefit from a required program of study by saying the college cannot *absolutely* prove its program is the best. It is, in short, the "relativistic" fallacy, ever popular in the twentieth century.

Saying there is no absolute knowledge in education is not the same as saying any and all claims to knowledge and judgment are of identical or equal value. Yes, a college may "err" in requiring students to study a given course, whatever that means, but the ability of a college's faculty to choose programs of study is superior to that of students because the faculty can bring learning and educational experience to bear on the question, and the ability of students to do so is immeasurably less. It is the difference between learned, experienced choice, and ignorant, naïve choice. The latter of course is not being "choice" in any meaningful use of the term but an example of skewed, callow or haphazard selection.

The only "mistake" the faculty can make regarding required courses is in *not* exercising its capacity to make demands on students based upon the faculty's learning and experience. The faculties of different colleges will not agree, of course, on the same programs of required general study. They will not, because learning, experience and judgment differ among the faculties of the more than 3,000 colleges in the U.S.

One result of colleges choosing different programs of required education, however, will be a number of approaches which can be tested against each other over time, as they have in fact been in the past, and altered according to what is learned in that experience. The result is a pluralism of thoughtful, vigorous and rigorous approaches to the best education possible. If this is embarrassing, it is an embarrassment of richness that will benefit society and culture.

There is surely more than one specific program of general education that can teach students to think about and appreciate the world in the manner of the learned disciplines, and thus to mature in their intellectual and judgmental capacities.

The *practical* objections to having required programs of general education are more numerous. It is difficult, it is said, to find large numbers of faculty who can teach interdisciplinary courses. This is true. But the more fundamental problem is in finding large numbers of faculty who can teach required courses in their respective disciplines and give students an understanding of how to think in those disciplines as well as to impart to students the contents of the courses in question. Both are a challenge to faculty to sharpen their teaching and their thinking. In other words, the demand is that faculty continue to advance their own educations, and this is precisely as it should be. Few things are as devastating to the enterprise of higher education, to students, society and culture, as the professor who is stagnating intellectually, or more common, the professor who is moving only *within* a narrow specialization, as is made possible when professors teach only elective courses in narrow specialties.

The professor who knows all there is to know about mining techniques in seventeenth century Mongolia and nothing else, and thus cannot relate what he knows to anything else, is of little use to himself, or to anyone else. The same is true of the specialist in computer science, twentieth century politics, economics, business management or any more popular, "less esoteric" specialty. Any specialty that is known and taught as an isolated content is "esoteric" in the basic and most important meaning of the term— its connections to our lives are unseen.

5.

Governance
and Constituents

IN 1984, the University Senate at the University of Minnesota voted on
a motion to eliminate most student memberships from the Senate, which
has legislative control over *all* university-wide educational matters. Student memberships, constituting one-third of the Senate, were added to
the body in 1969 after months of protest by students. The protests were
typical of the time. "I remember walking out of a meeting," says Professor Patricia Swan, "and seeing students stripped to the waist, painted red
like blood, blocking the exits."

The vote to return the Senate, and the university's educational authority, back to the faculty needed a two-thirds majority to pass. Student members of the Senate objected mainly on two grounds. One was the shop-
worn but still extremely popular argument of misplaced democracy that
confuses political representation, power and legitimacy with scholarly and
educational competence.

One student senator in 1984 quoted the written rationale given in 1969
to the cave-in to protestors' demands: "In an institution which considers
'the search for truth' its mission and exists within a society based on
democratic principles, no one segment, or group of segments, should determine the institution's full potential for the attainment of the truth."

"Look at that," the student exclaimed. "the report reads like it comes
from the Declaration of Independence. It says everything that democracy
stands for."

Predictably, the motion to return educational authority to the faculty was voted down. As one faculty participant wrote to me, "Not only did the students [as a bloc] vote against the loss of their membership, but many faculty members noted how difficult it was for them to take a position that seemed unfriendly to students, and they also voted against our resolution."

Another student senator stated a second objection, claiming the real motive behind the motion lay in a struggle between the faculty and the administration. He spoke of the the administration of the university assuming more and more power, and claimed the motion against the students was an attempt by a frustrated faculty to reclaim some of its power (not to say legitimate authority) over educational affairs.

Whatever the particular truth at the University of Minnesota, the second student was correct in asserting that academic authority, disastrously shared by the faculty with students since the Vietnam War period, is now being usurped by college presidents. There is a dangerous trend of conceiving of colleges not as collegial institutions but as analogous to business corporations, and of transforming college presidents into "Chief Executive Officers" (CEOs). The differences between a chief executive officer and a college president as a chief administrative officer are much more than merely semantic. A CEO formulates and dictates policy; a college president used to implement policy decided by others. Ironically, the powerful movement in the direction of the CEO model comes at a time when the abilities of college presidents to function in the tasks for which they are already responsible is being called into question, with good reason.

In 1984, a report was issued of a two-and-a-half year study by a commission of the Association of Governing Boards of Universities and Colleges. The commission, headed by former University of California President Clark Kerr, was not opposed to the CEO model of college presidencies. On the contrary, it was committed to it, and sought to advance it by advice on how college presidents could be more effective within that model—the group called itself the Commission on Strengthening Presidential Leadership. As it did so, however, the commission unwittingly gave practical reasons why the CEO design doesn't work and cannot work, even if we were to put aside the objection that the CEO model violates the essential relationship between *collegial* responsibility, educational quality, scholarly competence and academic freedom.

The Kerr Commission pronounced that "many presidents are better than the positions they hold." This is strange logic, for how are presidents known to be "better" except by evaluating how they function? And it is made even stranger by the Commission's finding that "about one-fourth of all presidents are quite satisfied with their situations (some are even euphoric); about one-half are clearly more satisfied than dissatisfied most of the time." (*Parentheses in the original.*)

The Kerr Commission also found, however, that presidents are "less engaged in making long-term plans and in preparing their institutions for the long-run future than they were in earlier times." The commission cited the fact that the average tenure of office of college presidents is only seven years. Instead of providing leadership, the Commission found that presidents "kind of go along day by day and wanting to last as long as they can."

The president-as-CEO bias of the Commission is shown when it cites as a major reason for the poor leadership of college presidents the fact that presidents of *public* colleges have a particularly difficult job because in most states they are required by "sunshine" laws to conduct their official business in open meetings. The Commission's evident preference is for presidents whose performance is hidden from scrutiny.

Among other constraints on presidents cited by the Kerr Commission is allegedly high faculty influence on faculty appointments. This is a startling assertion. The once respected faculty prerogative of appointing faculty has been greatly weakened since the 1960s by the increased influence on campuses of administrators, and even of students and boards of trustees, on faculty appointments.

In the same year, 1984, a survey by the *Chronicle of Higher Education* found that college presidents are spending "more time away from campuses." More than two-thirds of presidents surveyed complained that fund raising takes more of their time than ever before, as do endless meetings with government officers and others. "'Selling' the institution," wrote one president, "has become the first priority—to legislators, taxpayers, students, alumni, the community." Another said, "The job of CEO is becoming much more difficult, a no-win situation." Still another wrote that the job "has moved more and more in the direction of 'crisis management' at the expense of long-term management."

How in fact do college presidents function as managers of endless crises? According to some speakers at a conference on the question of

"Ethics in Higher Education" held in the summer of 1985 by the American Association of University Administrators, some college presidents cope by *lying*. They lie, it was said, to people both on and off campus. Said George A. Drake, President of Grinnell College, "I don't think you can be head of an institution and always tell the truth. If you think you're always going to tell the whole truth and nothing but the truth, you'll go crazy." Tulane President Eamon M. Kelly explained that presidents "have enormous opportunities to fabricate or lie. The only way to promote integrity is to say the same thing day after day, to every constituency."

A more accurate depiction would say that college presidents do not so much lie as speak vaguely, obliquely, not to the point, and that they withhold information, in order to cope with the myriad, contrasting and conflicting groups and individuals with whom they deal. In other words, the highly political nature of presidents' jobs has created for them a premium on the art of dissembling. It isn't a defect in in their individual characters that is being alleged. Rather it is a matter of the character of their careers determining their behavior.

Thus, by dissembling, college presidents alienate themselves more from the faculty, whose professional training and continuing work as scholars and teachers means they live daily in the ethics of scholarship and teaching. Those ethics place a premium on communicating clearly, openly, completely and precisely. Needless to say, the dissemblance of college presidents also puts off all those in the larger society who look for and who value straightforward communication from educators.

The vacuum in academic authority and integrity inherited from the late 1960s and early 1970s was first incompetently filled by students and more recently poorly filled by presidents. That authority is now being converted also by trustees. The traditional role of trustees was to oversee broadly understood, basic policy questions, and the financial integrity of colleges. Trustees refrained from interference either in the educational decisions of colleges or in their daily operations. This is no longer the case.

The situation was stated at a 1985 meeting of the Association of American Colleges by Spelman College President Donald M. Stewart, who said that trustees of American colleges are "really chomping at the bit to get at the problems that seem to lie in the academic areas," and that reports are calling for "a great deal of involvement on the part of trustees in academic programs." "I'm not sure," President Stewart concluded, "faculties are going to have the luxury of doing their own thing in this area for much longer."

President Stewart referred in particular to a publication of the Association of Governing Boards, entitled *Trustee Responsibility for Academic Affairs*. It states:

> Considerable uncertainty and ambiguity exist about lay participation in such a sensitive, professional domain. Faculty and administrators remind trustees now and then that academic affairs are the heart of the institution and that trustees should not attempt to function as specialists...[But the] realization that academic affairs constitutes the core of an institution can tempt boards to err in the opposite direction...Too much involvement by trustees can be construed as overstepping their policy-making role—substituting their judgement for that of faculty and administrators...[But] too little participation, on the other hand, can be construed as an evasion of responsibility.

The change of phraseology here is all-significant. In the past, there was the traditional, strong standard that there should be *no* "trustee involvement in academic affairs." In fact the change parallels and complements the change of the traditional, absolute, unqualified "faculty governance of academic affairs" before the mid-1960s, to the phrase used since then of "faculty *participation* in governance of academic affairs."

But we don't have to infer what powers *Trustee Responsibility for Academic Affairs* advocates for trustees. It states them baldly:

> Despite the potential discomfort,...[trustees] should question administrators about program priorities: Which programs best support the institution's missions and strategies? Which programs are central? Which are peripheral? Which programs are likely to grow? Which are likely to decline? Which programs are vital to the institution's mission? How are we preparing for anticipated changes in the environment? What are our competitive advantages and disadvantages?

Even an unguarded reading of this proposed role reveals it is a formula for turning the most important decisions about academic affairs over to trustees. For what is more important than decisions about what academic programs are "central" or not to a college's "mission"? And making academic decisions based on "enrollment trends" and "competitive advantages" begs the question of liberal education backed by firm academic authority versus servile education.

It should be clear by now that the question, and indeed the current crisis, of governance is central to the most fundamental issues about higher education. It is not just a question of means, although it is commonly perceived as such. (The false separation of "means" and "ends" is another of the disastrous dualisms that perennially plague higher education.)

Coming to the central and most critical of college constituencies, the faculty, we see, 1) too much acceptance by them of the ends versus means dualism, and, 2) a near fatal loss of confidence in their own governing role over academic affairs. This is so even as administrators and trustees are successfully completing the wresting of academic authority away from faculty that began with the student usurpations of the late 1960s and the early 1970s.

Still another report, *Faculty Participation in Decision Making* (known as the "Floyd Report" after its author, Carol E. Floyd), by the Washington-based Clearing House on Higher Education, found that although faculty still think their role in governance is critical, and regard academic decisions made by those other than the faculty as not "legitimate," and even resist implementing them, too many faculty *do not and will not take part in governance*. Usurpation of faculty authority by others is a disease that feeds upon itself. This is so not only, as we have seen, by all the other constituents being emboldened by their success to take more of governance away from the faculty. The loss of faculty authority to students, administrators and trustees has also resulted in a loss of faculty confidence in their governing responsibility, and hence a shunning of that responsibility. "The most marked declines in faculty morale," says the Floyd Report, "have been found at institutions where faculty perceive that their role in institutional governance and planning has been significantly reduced."

Here we come to the crux of the matter. Perhaps *the* major cause of the malaise of higher education is the weakened position and morale of the faculty. The New Left and counterculture reformers of the Vietnam period were so successful in assaulting the authority of the faculty that a serious gap was left in academic affairs. Today, ironically, the gap is being filled by off-campus big business and big foundations, and on campus by administrators and trustees. The coalition of administrators and big corporations is sidestepping the faculty, and in many cases ignoring them altogether in reforms made since the mid-1980s.

The most powerful off-campus, nongovernmental group focusing on reform in higher education today is the Business-Higher Education Forum. The Forum meets several times a year and issues expensively published reports, distributed free of charge to influential recipients. (As one high-living officer of a large, powerful New York City-based foundation once quipped to me when I remarked that the foundation's executive dining room was as opulent as that of New York's luxurious Four Seasons Restaurant, "Ah, the humanities and the amenities, they go together.") The Forum's reports contain recommendations for colleges and universities.

The Forum is made up of the chief executive officers from major corporations such as RCA, General Electric, General Motors, 3M Corporation, Westinghouse and Rockwell International. These men and companies who now seek to shape higher education in the guise of "making the U.S. more competitive economically" vis-á-vis other nations are the same people whose lack of vision in their own sphere caused American business to fall behind the economies of Japan, West Germany, Korea, Taiwan, Singapore and Brazil, especially in research, design and other product innovations, and in marketing. Fresh from its failures in business, corporate America is now turning its competence on higher education.

Joining the CEOs of the corporate elite in the Forum are the "CEOs," i.e., the presidents and other high ranking administrators, of major colleges and universities. Among those on the long list are the presidents of the University of Notre Dame, the University of Chicago, Georgetown University, Radcliffe College, the California Institute of Technology and Washington University. There is a third category of members of the Forum —politicians (not surprisingly), including several members of the U.S. Congress. Even Art Buchwald, listed as "Humorist," was a primary speaker at one of the conferences of the Forum.

What is sadly humorous is that the meetings and conferences of the Forum rarely include a single faculty member from any college or university. The Forum's highly influential efforts to shape higher education according to its lights are comparable to an attempt to reform medicine without including doctors among the reformers. The Forum's activities are the leading edge of big business's pressure to turn out students with "marketable skills," turning colleges into career and vocational schools little concerned with the social and ethical aspects of these careers and vocations, to say nothing of any substantial liberal education of students' minds and characters.

That big business has been joined by presidents of top colleges and universities is not surprising. The individual presidents' careers depend on "bringing home the bacon," i.e., on bringing back to their institutions the grants that big corporations promise (and sometimes deliver). Nor are many presidents at all adverse to having the powerful off-campus support of real CEOs in their drive to become CEOs themselves. For their part, the corporation CEOs express a desire to deal with their "peers" on campuses, meaning college presidents, and decidedly not with faculty. The corporation chiefs do not understand the essential, collegial nature of universities, or are indifferent or hostile to it.

That the trend to take education out of the hands of educators and place it under the control of administrators and their off-campus "peers" is a mania can be seen also in a report about the college at which I am a professor. In the academic year of 1985-86, a committee of the Middle States Association of Colleges and Schools (MSACS) did its periodic evaluation of Queens College (CUNY)—a standard practice. The MSACS report states that although Queens College is very seriously underfunded, the quality of education at the college is excellent. The report *explicitly* attributes the educational excellence to what it terms the extraordinarily high level of faculty governance and faculty morale at the college. Then, in a leap beyond all logic, the MSACS report goes on to recommend that much of the governance of the college should be surrendered by the faculty to the college's president.

Consistent with the puzzling reasoning of the MSACS committee is the fact that on the national level faculty morale is at an all time low. The poor conditions under which faculty operate have been instrumental in keeping them in a weakened position, and keeping them from revitalizing and regaining more of their former status and primary role in directing higher education. In addition to still being debilitated by the Vietnam War period's "reforms," we are not yet out of a time of decreasing enrollments of the traditional students between the ages seventeen to twenty-two (a result of the demographics of the "baby boom" generation having passed through colleges), and cost-cutting measures in colleges, with consequent layoffs of younger, untenured faculty. Professorial positions won't open up until the mid-1990s when the predominantly middle-aged faculty of today will start to retire or die in large numbers.

One of higher education's cost-saving devices has been the widespread use of "adjunct" or part-time faculty. Today, part-timers teach 41 percent of all college classes in the U.S. This has created a class of exploited faculty, deplored as *"Untermenschen"* by the City University of New York's Chancellor Joseph S. Murphy. Indeed the widespread exploitation of adjuncts by colleges is one of higher education's dirtiest secrets. The rejoinder of some college presidents that the adjuncts are people successful in other careers who only "moonlight" in college teaching is spurious, as is shown in a 1986 survey by the League for Innovation in Community Colleges. The survey found that 50 percent of part timers teaching at community colleges said they would accept full-time faculty positions if they are offered to them. And it should be noted that community colleges, because of their high orientation toward vocational education, are *more* likely to use moonlighters who are successful in other careers than are four-year colleges. Conversely, it is a good assumption that many more than 50 percent of the adjuncts at four-year colleges would accept full-time positions.

Adjuncts are paid on an hourly basis, which, assuming a full teaching load only possible by teaching at two or more colleges (in fact not the case with most adjuncts), provides an *annual* income of some $6,000 to $10,000. The official poverty level for a family of four as defined by the U.S. government is $10,000 in annual income. The adjuncts have no health benefits, are hired on a semester-to-semester basis, accumulate no seniority, have no say in the governance of departments or colleges, and, of course, are in jobs which do not lead to tenure or promotion.

Most important, the overuse of adjuncts also cheats students. The part-timers' presence on campuses and their availability to students are minimal, their opportunity to conduct research and increase their knowledge in their respective fields (hard to do when you're driving a cab) is limited. Understandably, their overall state of mind and energy while on campus is poor.

Coming back to the state of *full-time* faculty, their income in terms of real purchasing power declined 20 percent from 1970 to 1983. One professor lamented, "I have a younger brother—he's 31, ten years younger than I—and he went to work for a Fortune 500 company. Would you believe he's making five times my salary? His bonus this year was larger than my entire annual salary."

The average annual salary for full-time faculty at four-year colleges in the 1985-86 academic year was $26,920. The average for full professors was $34,280. For the more numerous associate professors it was $27,600. The still more numerous assistant professors averaged $22,980, lecturers $21,910, and instructors $18,730.

Especially galling to those who work to restore high-quality education is the fact that faculty who teach the liberal arts are paid less than the average. To put it conversely, two 1986 studies (by the College and University Personnel Association and the American Association of State Colleges and Universities) showed that faculty in "high demand" fields are getting salaries that average as much as 30 percent above salaries for others in their ranks. In order of highest averages are the fields of engineering, business and accounting. All this encourages servile rather than liberal education.

A cynical "star" system is being developed by some colleges, and it is further eroding faculty morale and jeopardizing the future of a high-quality faculty in American higher education. These schools are raiding the faculties of other colleges by recruiting prestigious professors at special, higher salaries. The raiding schools get instant prestige on the cheap, but almost all of their students continue to be taught by underpaid, overworked faculty. The University of California at Irvine has paid $76,000 in annual salaries to get ten specific professors, while the University of Tennessee at Knoxville has paid $85,000 each for three engineering professors. George Mason University pays annual salaries of $60,000 to $123,000 to recruit faculty stars. The Dean of Science at M.I.T. summed up the practice by saying, as quoted by *Time* magazine: "A lot of universities are out to buy a professor." This at a time when 40 percent of all of America's 500,000 college faculty will have to be replaced by the year 1995 and 80 percent in twenty years, when starting salaries for assistant professors average $20,000, and when only three-tenths of 1 per cent of college freshmen indicate they would like a career as college professors.

In the light of this picture, it is not surprising that a 1984 Carnegie Foundation survey found that 50 percent of college faculty nationwide said they would not recommend an academic career to their students. Fifty-four percent felt that administrators at their respective institutions are insensitive to their research needs. Sixty-three percent rate the overall performance of administrators at their respective institutions as only fair to poor. And 50 percent said they are very apprehensive about the future of higher education. The 1984 Carnegie report concluded by warning that low salaries, inadequate working conditions and poor morale may prevent higher education from adequately filling, with high-quality people, the estimated 400,000 faculty openings over the next twenty years. As mentioned, this figure represents 80 percent of all college faculty in the U.S.

Another study of college faculty was conducted from 1983 to 1986 by Howard R. Bowen and Jack H. Schuster. Entitled *American Professors: A Natural Resource Imperiled,* it directly identifies poor working conditions as one cause of faculty depression. The authors found that "at two-thirds of the campuses we visited faculty morale seemed to be no better than fair, and at a quarter of the campuses we characterized morale as 'very poor.' Our best characterization of faculty morale is 'shaky.'" The reasons the authors cited for this situation were declining real-term salaries, and "deterioration in the faculty's working conditions...from diminishing clerical support to increasingly obsolete [laboratory] instrumentation, from negligible travel allowances to poorly prepared students."

Bowen and Schuster, unlike so many other critics of higher education, correctly perceive that any reform movement must address professorial discontent in order to be effective. They say:

> Nor do the recent, well-publicized reports advocating the rehabilitation of undergraduate education adequately address the plight of liberal arts faculty. For the most part, faculty are perceived as clinging to entrenched interests that must be counteracted in order to achieve educational reform. However too little is made of the adverse circumstances in which many faculty members now find themselves. By underemphasizing the condition of the professoriate, proponents of educational reform neglect the variable most necessary for infusing the liberal arts with new vitality. All who are committed to the proposition that liberal learning should be the nucleus of our curricula must squarely confront a number of faculty related issues linked to our ability to educate liberally.

A perfect example of misdirected efforts to reform higher education is reflected in the continuing debate over the amount of time professors should devote to research versus teaching. Several reports, among them the National Endowment for the Humanities Report, personally authored by then Secretary of Education William J. Bennett, and the Report of the Association of American Colleges, set serious research in opposition to good teaching, reasoning that the time and energy required for research inevitably draws these resources away from the classroom.

Pitting teaching against research leads to two recommendations that are being strongly urged and whose primary purpose, in my opinion, is cost-cutting, still again at the expense of quality education. One recommendation is to increase faculty teaching loads, making it more difficult for professors to pursue scholarship and research. The second is the "two-tiered" approach, that is, to create two formal classes of college faculty: researchers who would do no teaching, and teachers who would do no research. The knowledge gained by the researchers would, thus, not provide essential first-hand enrichment to students in the classroom. And the nonscholar teachers would depend on second-hand scholarship for use in the classroom, at best. The latter would be in fact high school teachers, and the quality of education their students would receive would be at that level. High school teaching is a perfectly honorable profession, needing and deserving of respect. But what would be the good purposes of turning colleges into high schools?

Furthermore, the efforts of these reformers run directly contrary to the realities of professional life on campus. Love of scholarship and love of teaching are almost always two aspects of the same passion. In my experience in college teaching since 1961, every professor reported by students to be a poor teacher has also had a poor record of scholarship. While not every serious scholar I've encountered has been dynamite in the classroom, most display a love and dedication for their subject which can be infectious to any student who is open to learning.

The pressure to turn college professors into mere "employees," and to turn most of them into de facto high school teachers, ironically comes at a time when many of those who have studied *high school* education are recommending that teachers at that level be given governance of academic affairs at their schools, meaning of course, that governance be taken out of the hands of the administrators, in this case high school principals. For the good of education, it is being recommended that high school teachers be given the governance role traditionally enjoyed by college faculty at the very same time that enormous pressures are being brought to bear to take that authority away from the college faculty—another example of the topsy-turvy thinking about higher education begun in the 1960s and still crippling the enterprise. In 1986, a report entitled *A Nation Prepared* recommended that high schools should "be run by teachers...just as law firms are run by lawyers." "Lead teachers," the report recommended, should run the high schools, *instead* of administrators, i.e., principals. A "partnership of teachers" would replace the present hierarchical structure of high schools dominated by principals

As noted, the powerful efforts to turn college presidents into "chief executive officers"—and we have seen that indeed the very term is being applied to presidents by themselves and others—is being pushed by big business, which has formed alliances with college administrators. The CEO posture suits both the more narrow interests of administrators and the biases of some powerful business CEOs, who, it is said, "are more comfortable dealing with equals rather than professors." (Of course, in the consciousness of many may be the thought, "If a bunch of rag tag hippies grabbed power over academic affairs away from the professors in the 60s and 70s, then, hell, anyone can do it. And why not us?")

What these corporate executives fail to understand or choose to ignore is that there is a critical difference between the lateral, power-sharing nature of collegial institutions and the vertical or pyramid power structure of business organizations. By nature a collegial institution is one in which decisions are made by a large number of professionals in deliberation with each other, engaging in an open process that takes time and patience. The minutest details are often disputed, so the process can often appear not only glacially slow, but petty as well. Yet, it is this very process that is absolutely essential to academic freedom, integrity and quality. The process can be easily viewed with impatience, unfortunately even by many of today's faculty who have become attuned to an "activist" society. And the collegial process is easily caricatured as debating questions of angels dancing on the head of a pin by appealing to the anti-intellectual currents which have always been and still are present in our society.

Traditionally, college presidents were considered "chief educators among equals." Their role began to change after World War II. A galaxy of conditions, among them rising college costs and an explosion in numbers of students, led them to become first mere managers, then fund raisers, public relations people, professional socializers and crisis managers. It was this transformation of the presidents from educators to a jacks-of-all-practical-trades that helped create their present poor influence on academic

91

authority and quality. So the aforementioned 1984 report of the Commission on Strengthening Presidential Leadership, a commission friendly to presidents in general and to their posture as CEOs in particular, found that colleges lack leadership from their presidents. The job of college president, the commission determined, is too constrained by outside influences, too stressful, diverse and fragmented, and thus too unrewarding to attract the most qualified people.

Furthermore presidencies do not carry tenure and, as noted, today the average presidential term is only about seven years. College presidents can be compared to rods who catch lightning from all directions, ranging from the local dog warden (the question of students keeping pets has become a perennial problem on campuses since colleges gave up their *in loco parentis* authority) to state legislators and federal agencies, to the press, and to literally innumerable pressure groups and individuals. Resisting pressures to accommodate or appease educationally unsound demands frequently requires more wisdom, stamina and courage than it is reasonable to expect any single individual to possess.

Complicating the situation is the fact that the very nature of the college presidency as it has grown over the past forty years doesn't allow those who hold it time to read or reflect, an essential requirement to sound deliberation of educational questions. Presidents are usually yoked to endless hours of public relations, human relations, crisis resolving and fund raising responsibilities. While these are valuable services to colleges and universities, they are also consuming. A ridiculous amount of presidents' time is taken up by what former Yale president Angelo Bartlett Giamatti once characterized to me as "gorgeous routine," exemplified by his having to sign about 150 letters per day.

The problems inherent in today's presidencies are difficult to reconcile with the long-term integrity of colleges and universities, and the quality of education they offer. Not surprisingly, they also skewer presidents' perceptions. Studies conducted in the mid-1980s by the Carnegie Foundation and *The Chronicle of Higher Education* found that although 80 percent of faculty felt they did not have ample opportunity to influence academic policies at their respective institutions, only 4 percent of college presidents perceived governance as a major issue of concern. And over 60 percent of presidents rated the climate for higher education as "excellent" or "good," in sharp contrast to every other group that has expressed itself on the subject since 1983.

The structure of colleges is changing, just as surely as the roles of their presidents, as the institutions are forced to dovetail more and more with outside institutions, private and governmental. From the private sector, the expectations of corporations to deal with campus "CEOs" is but part of the larger demand that colleges be run like corporations. That is, the pressures are not only that authority in colleges be centralized, but also that colleges adopt business values like cost-efficiency (if not profit), competition with other institutions, and near exclusive attention to these and other short-term goals—the last being one of the very modes of thought that has made American corporations so noncompetitive vis-á-vis foreign companies.

From another side, as governmental agencies—federal, state and local—regulate and oversee colleges (always claiming the best of intentions), the colleges restructure themselves, and the nature and quality of education they offer, to reflect the multiple agencies with which they have to deal. (The notion that form and function are separable is still another of the false dualisms plaguing education.) So colleges are becoming ever-more bureaucratized.

Colleges are increasingly molded and fettered by regulations and by those who formulate and enforce regulations. They are forced to squander their mental, physical and financial resources on the bureaucrats and their rules within and outside the colleges. And the malaise feeds upon itself. The occupational *raison d'etre* of bureaucrats depends on their ever maintaining and expanding rules, regulations and other red tape. Thus the administrations of colleges come to reflect more and more—and in fact to a large extent become inseparable from—external and internal bureaucracies. As this has happened, the traditional and once healthy tensions between administrators and faculty have become frictions between groups serving radically incompatible aims.

In 1986, events took place at Dartmouth College that are intriguing in their precedent-setting possibilities. The president of the school, David McLaughlin, a former CEO of the Toro lawnmowing machine company, had been a CEO going at full-steam. Among other accomplishments, he had raised Dartmouth's endowments from $254 million to $414 million, increased average faculty salaries by 33.7 percent, and increased black enrollment to 9 percent. Nevertheless, he ran afoul of the faculty because, in the words of Professor of Biology Melvin Speigel, "He responds as chairman of the board, not as president and leader of this institution."

A special faculty committee at Dartmouth wrote a report charging that "The administration of the college is insensitive to and not knowledgeable about educational concerns and [the faculty's] proper and necessary role in the governance of the college." To be sure, the grievances of some of the faculty went beyond this to complaints involving political questions, and thus the issues in the conflict became somewhat muddled. President McLaughlin was accused of being soft on students who tore down shanties erected on campus by other students to protest Dartmouth's investments in companies doing business in South Africa. Still, the faculty confrontation with the president was effective. President McLaughin conceded that he "learned a good lesson," and that he "did not take the time for the deliberative processes of the college."

In the world of higher education on the whole, the schisms continue to widen between faculty and educational concerns on the one hand and administrations and bureaucratic hegemony on the other. In the process, academic authority, academic judgment, academic independence, academic morale and academic quality all continue to slide below their present alarming depressions. In these declines, nadirs are not yet in sight, despite, and in part *because of,* all the (mostly misconceived) pressures to reform higher education in the late 1980s.

6.

The Open Society, Social Justice, and Power

THERE ARE THREE truths that should be regarded as truisms in the university. But today many academicians do not even see them as true. This is more evidence of the dire crisis in which higher education is foundering. These truths are: 1) the open society is one that tolerates, invites, protects and values the critical faculties of individuals. 2) justice exists for individuals or it exists not at all. And 3) the well-being of both the open society and justice depends on the free, critical faculties of citizens being developed through education.

The knot of openness, justice and liberal education is being hacked at by swords of power and ideology, slashed in fierce cross-strokes by would-be Alexanders of commercialism and the political New Left. Both aim the sharpest cuts of all at higher education, a major life-line holding together a free, developed and open society and civilization. Openness and justice can falter but still be saved through the results of liberal education, the application of free and cultivated critical faculties of individuals. But the weakening or extinction of citizens' free and developed critical faculties themselves would doom any open and just society. And it is in this very direction that combined forces of the New Left and commercialism push us.

One of the great misunderstandings of our time is that the commitment to free and open society, and the liberal education that is its *sine qua non,* is a "middle of the road" position, an intellectually wan midway between the doctrinaire New Left and "practical," anti-intellectual commercialism. The reality is to the contrary. The position of liberal education and a free and open society is antipodes apart from both. It may be graphically symbolized thus:

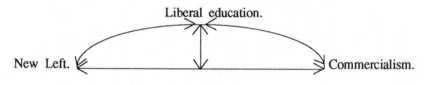

Liberal education.

New Left.   Commercialism.

Servile Education.

The New Left despises academically free, liberal education. It favors politicized education to achieve its notions of domestic and international "justice." The commercialists, on the other hand, would overturn liberal education in the name of mammon and "the national interest."

Commercialism appeals to powerful but transparent aspects of our nature—fear, materialism and greed. But the New Left's invocation of justice purports to appeal to the highest within us—our humanity and moral sensibility. The New Left's strength, and the danger it presents, then, are exponentially compounded. Its danger is insidious and also intractable because it acts principally from within the academy. For nowhere has the New Left so taken root as in our universities, specifically with many faculty members, especially (but not exclusively) among many who were themselves students in the 1960s and 1970s when the New Left grossly threw its weight around on American campuses.

The New Left's aim is to make higher education servile to schemes of justice antithetical to the free and open society, and to liberal education and academic freedom which nurture that society. The New Left's position has been frankly stated many times in the past two decades and more. For example, shortly after the dawn of the movement, Alan Wolfe declared the New Left's academic and social credo in the July 1969 issue of *Center Magazine*:

The social [politicized] university is not primarily concerned with the abstract pursuit of scholarship, but with the utilization of knowledge obtained through scholarship to obtain social change. Therefore it does not recognize the right of its members to do anything they wish under the name of academic freedom: instead it assumes that all its members are committed to social change. To give an example, a course in riot control would simply be out of place in such a university, while a course in methods of rioting might be perfectly appropriate.

The New Left today seeks to achieve its goal on campuses by several means:

1. By turning individual courses and the curriculum as a whole into indoctrination about alleged evils of the United States, evils concealed behind its fraudulent mask of democracy, which also disguises the violence underlying the facade. Unlike education, indoctrination aims not at a balanced, impartial view of subject matter, but at a deliberately biased one. As an illustration, one of my students reported to me about two years ago that a teacher had begun a course on American foreign policy by saying, "In this course, I'm going to teach you why the Third World hates the United States." And at least as important, as noted, unlike education which simply requires that the student *understand* what is being taught, indoctrination requires that the student *believe* what he is taught and that he give his intellectual and moral loyalty to it—and in the case of the New Left his political loyalty as well.

Another student, a young woman, reported that her teacher, a self-styled radical feminist, punished her for saying that one of her major goals in life was to marry and have children. The punishment? The student was told that in order to pass the course, one in communications, she would have to present the teacher with evidence that she had participated during the semester in pro-feminist activism of some kind acceptable to the teacher. The student elected to drop the course and not initiate a complaint against the teacher—not a surprise since the student was a nineteen year-old sophomore and the teacher a formidable personality about forty years of age.

2. By teaching that the university should be an instrument for achieving a revolution in the United States. The New Left has not become much more precise about the society to be created by its revolution than it was in the 1960s when it claimed the goal would come out of the revolution itself rather than be defined before it. At times, some New Leftists call themselves "Marxists," but their analyses of things are so wooly-minded they are at best nominally Marxist rather than substantively and recog-

nizably so. The same is true of New Leftists' claims to be socialists—one is usually hard pressed to find the socialist structure in their thoughts.

What the New Left *is* clear about are assertions that the United States is fundamentally and incorrigibly evil in its political and economic structures. The claim of the New Left is that the U.S. is a corporate state which oppresses racial and ethnic minorities, women, labor, homosexuals and youth. The New Left used to call the nation *Amerika*, the Germanic spelling meant to connote Nazism/facism. The term has been dropped, but the charge remains the same. Civil and human rights progress in the U.S. is given scant attention, except for being demeaned as the desperate concessions of an oppressive "system," "establishment" or "power structure" to stave off the goal of total revolution.

As it did with students, blacks, and others during the Vietnam/Civil Rights period, the New Left gains mileage from popular sentiments in the country. Today there is a feeling on the part of many Americans that the country is too obsessed with communism, or too militarily muscle-bound, or too compromised by its economic interests, or too stupid, to play any constructive role in the world, especially one that involves the use of economic hegemonic power or military force.

In the New Left's view, the U.S. is seen only as the provocateur of Communist nations and the exploiter of Third World countries. In its political thrust *per se*, this stance has led to a new isolationism in the U.S. The *old* isolationism of the political *right* in the 1930s saw the U.S. as too good to be involved in a dirty world. The new isolationism inspired by the New Left portrays the U.S. as too evil or stupid to be allowed involvement in international affairs—except of course to accede in the demands and acquiesce in the actions to the Second (Communist) World and the Third World. The domestic thrust of this self-hating isolationism is to destroy Western culture and institutions at home, higher education being a central target because it conspicuously represents Western culture, which, in turn, greatly depends on it.

As noted, the premise of the new isolationism is the contrary of that of the old isolationism of the 1930s that saw the U.S. as too good to get involved with the world, but today's isolationism comes down to same kind of unreasoning opposition to U.S. involvement with anything beyond its borders. Except that the New Left incessantly pushes for U.S. intervention to overthrow right-wing or racist regimes, e.g., the Shah's Iran, Marcos' Philippines, the apartheid regime in South Africa, almost as strongly as it objects to the U.S. opposing any action whatsoever against leftist or Communist regimes or movements. And the New Left excuses Communist aggressions on the basis that they spread needed revolution against right wing states, e.g., Cuba's and Nicaragua's support of the Communist guerillas in El Salvador, or as the legitimate need to gain buffer states against possible Western aggression, e.g., the USSR's invasion and atrocious suppression of Afghanistan.

The sins of Third World governments are ignored altogether by the New Left in a long pattern running from Nigeria's systematic starvation of its Biafran minority to Pol Pot's systematic genocide against the Cambodian population. The bad faith follows from the intense loyalty to the New Left's intellectually sloppy but emotionally virulent hatred of the West and of its values.

3. By taking the privileged position of academicians and using it to violate and otherwise show contempt for the values the privilege is meant to protect. So New Left faculty have no trouble accepting tenure but oppose academic freedom that the institution of tenure is meant to protect. The opposition is sometimes rationalized by the claim that academic freedom and freedom of speech should be restricted to those who hold only correct views of "anti-imperialism," "anti-racism," "anti-male chauvinism," etc., all, of course, as defined by the New Left. In other words, the New Left labors to replace academic freedom and freedom of speech on campuses with required orthodox thinking.

Another New Left rationalization is that objective scholarship is not only undesirable, immoral and serves the evil status quo of America (a lingering version of "You're either part of the solution or part of the problem"), but that it is impossible. The schools are inevitably politicized, the rationale has it, so they should be so in favor of the correct ("revolutionary") political stances rather than the wrong ("reactionary") ones.

The argument is so weak that it would be laughable except that it convinces the already politicized, and they include many graduates of highly politicized colleges since the late 1960s, and some callow and gullible current students. It ignores the truth that a plurality of points of view among the faculty of a college presents the students with pluralism and a *de facto* balanced education. In addition, in its contemptuous dismissal of fair teaching as "false consciousness," to use an old Marxist term, the New Left glosses over the fact that faculty who are committed to seeking objective truth as far as is humanly possible according to the standards of an open system of evidence and argument are quite different in intent and consequence, despite their personal human weaknesses and biases, than those intent on indoctrination.

The New Left sees the universities as part of a structure supporting an American capitalist corporate state that is imperialistic abroad and is oppressive of labor, women, homosexuals, youth and ethnic and racial minorities at home. The system should be revolutionized, and one way to do so is to continue to revolutionize the university. In recent years, the movement, which has no tolerance for other points of view, and dismisses them as rationalizations of the corporate state and society, seeks to advance the revolution by capturing the curricula and classrooms of colleges, and to do away with academic objectivity and academic freedom. For example, Professor Bertell Ollman argues in *Regulating the Intellectuals* that academic freedom "may be part of the problem...because the ideal of academic freedom helps to disguise and distort an essentially repressive practice by presuming it as an imperfect version of what should be." There are echoes of Marcuse's "repressive tolerance" here.

Yet another tactic of the New Left is to fasten upon an up-to-date good cause, *multiculturalism* and *pluralism,* and use it as a vehicle in its program, just as the Vietnam War and the civil rights movement once served its purposes. A well-publicized example took place in the spring of 1988 at Stanford University, and has had repercussions on other campuses because of Stanford's prestige. Some five years before, Stanford, recovering from the 1960s and 1970s trashing of curricula, had reinstituted a required freshman course in Western Culture. In 1986, the course came under attack by a handful of students and faculty as "imperialistic," "sexist" and "racist" because the authors of the books on the reading list of the course were, in the words of one student, "all written by dead, white males." Stanford's president, Donald Kennedy, as has been the wont of college presidents when confronted by New Left demands since the mid-1960s, lent his voice to those calling for change.

Some faculty members defended the course on Western culture in terms that were reasoned, temperate and addressed to the educational values of the course. Those faculty members who defended the Western culture course were joined by the dean of Undergraduate Studies and, as a poll showed, the overwhelming majority of Stanford's students. They were denounced in viciously demagogic rhetoric. For example, the chairperson of the Black Student Union wrote, "These individuals are sending me, women and all women of color a message that says loud and clear 'niggers go home.' That is the battle cry of Howard Beach, N.Y., and that is what the Klan puts out everyday. 'We don't want your kind challenging our predominance and superiority.'"

A committee was set up to review the freshman course, and recommended expanding the course to include contributions of women and minorities to Western culture. However, on the day the Faculty Senate was to vote on the proposed reform, the Rev. Jesse Jackson, who had no affiliation with Stanford, led a noisy march on campus to the place where the Senate was meeting. The marchers chanted, "Hey, hey, ho, ho, Western culture's got to go!" (There is no record of the university's president or of the faculty protesting against Jackson's interference with Stanford's academic affairs. This would hardly have been the reaction, and should not have been the reaction, if a right-wing preacher, let's say a TV evangelist, had marched on the Faculty Senate.) Some protesting students let it be known that they would storm the room where the Senate was meeting and disrupt its session if it did not vote their way. The Senate caved in. It abolished the course in Western Culture and adopted the demanded substitute of a course on "Culture, Ideas, and Values." Some of the new course's advocates smirked on television as they dubbed it "CIV."

Gone from the new required course are such authors as Homer, Dante and Darwin. These will be replaced by works written by non-Europeans, chosen because they are non-Europeans, to be selected *ad hoc* by the course's instructors. In addition, all instructors of CIV are mandated to pay "substantial attention to issues of race, gender and class." Furthermore, there is no chronological order to the works to be studied, as if ideas have no history, no continuity and no evolution.

There are three sets of lessons to be learned from the Stanford experience. *One* is that the New Left's 1960s' tactic of intimidation by use of false charges of "racism," "sexism," "elitism," etc., are still effective, and their success at Stanford in 1988 ensured that the tactic was intensified on other American campuses. It takes exceptional courage to stand up to these vicious charges, which are calculated to close off reasonable debate and bully the majority of faculty into capitulation.

Two, the counterculture movement is far from dead, although its proponents no longer use the term, and the movement will be further emboldened to trash higher education by the events at Stanford. Indeed, in a follow-up on the Stanford story, *Time* magazine on 11 April 1988 reported that "At Pittsburgh's Carnegie-Mellon University, English Chairman Gary Waller assigns his classes the recent cult film *Blue Velvet* for comparisons with works by T.S. Eliot and William Butler Yeats."

Counterculture holds that Shakespeare's plays and comic books are of the same order. The New Left, in distinction, in its current guise of "deconstructionist" scholarship holds that the significance of Shakespeare's plays is that they are an expression of, if not a front for, the economic and political order of his time. For example, a panel of the American Council of Learned Societies in 1988 issued a report called *Speaking for the Humanities*. The report holds that Shakespeare's *The Tempest* "becomes even more powerful and complex when read in the context of colonial expeditions in which native populations...were enslaved and, often, tortured and killed." The panel which produced the report included the director of the Whitney Humanities Center at Yale, the director of the Society for the Humanities at Cornell, and the director of the Center for Literary and Cultural Studies at Harvard.

The *third* lesson is that the assault on higher education by the New Left and counterculture is not another example in American history of laudable or benign attempts to reform an outdated system, such as the movements before the 1960s I have reviewed in Chapter II. It differs in that it is part of a massive effort to destroy many of the central ideals of Western civilization as we know them, and higher education as a vital organ of those ideals.

The "milder" charge that requiring students to study Western culture is "imperialistic" because it implies a view that Western culture is better or superior to other cultures is spurious. As Professor Carl Degler pointed out during the Stanford debate, "We are part of the West because the language, religion, laws, customs, literature, yes, even the prejudices of this country were drawn overwhelmingly from Europe." In other words, we study Western culture not to glorify it or ourselves but to understand ourselves though understanding our common legacy. Nor is it true that there is a consensus, let alone a monolithic point of view, among the West's historical writers and thinkers. Far from it. And in further refutation of the charge that study of Western civilization leads to "parochialism," or "Eurocentricism," we need only note that courses and programs of study about non-Western cultures are available at Stanford and at most other colleges of any size. The same is true of ethnic and women's studies, both legitimate areas of study.

The pretense that the assault on Western civilization aimed at "inclusion," for example, of contributions by women and blacks to the West and by non-Western cultures to humanity, was seen to be false when the review committee at Stanford recommended these very kinds of inclusion by extending the course's requirements. This was rejected. The true aim of the assault was seen to be not inclusion but *exclusion,* exclusion of as much as possible of Western culture and its replacement by a politicized, anti-Western curriculum.

The choice of works to be read by the race, gender or nationality of their authors rather than the intrinsic merit of the works themselves is an illustration of political intents replacing educational ones. To be sure, Plato was a white, European male, but he raised questions in his works which are essential to all humans, and he did so with unsurpassed profundity and clarity. Furthermore, he did so in a historical context that must be understood if we are to understand Western civilization, without which we cannot comprehend its relations to other civilizations, current issues and perennial human questions. As Sidney Hook put it:

> One can distinguish for pedagological purposes between the study of a great work that contributes to the student's understanding of it as an expression of the culture of its time, its influence on subsequent generations including the present, and an analysis of the problems and questions it generates in contemporary society. Plato's *Republic* is a good instance. A skillful teacher can show how the problems of war, peace, social justice, feminism, education, and government are adumbrated in Plato's argument, but what is distinctive about Plato and Greek culture would be lost if *The Republic* were studied merely as a text in social problems which could be more fruitfully explored in other ways. Failure to recognize this distinction as well as the expectation that a course in Western culture can embrace all areas of social and political life is sure to generate misunderstanding. It will also overlook the perennial problems of philosophy, among them the definition and quest of a meaningful and satisfying life.

For these reasons as well, the purported mix-and-match approach to selection of works in Stanford's new CIV course is very inferior to the course replaced in providing a foundation upon which students can build a coherent, in-depth education.

The common-front assault by the New Left, counterculturists, the ignorant and commercialist forces is less raucous or violent than the attacks in the 1960s and 1970s, but it is very strong. The Stanford experience is paralleled in innumerable colleges, academic departments and academic committees. The situation at my own school is typical. A few years back, some required courses were reintroduced after a program of required courses had been abolished during the Vietnam War era. Now, courses in at least one non-Western civilization are required. But no systematic study of Western civilization is required of students. And as the events at Stanford illustrate, the enemies of higher education can turn as intimidating, slanderous and ugly as they did in the 1960s and 1970s when they deem it necessary to get their way. And all of it is done in the name of "social and international justice."

A temperately written, and highly influential, scholarly philosophy of social justice is found in John Rawls' *A Theory of Justice*. The 1971 book has influenced many on campuses. It provides a highly abstract and complicated argument for egalitarianism on nonpolitical grounds, and by doing so disposes people to accept the egalitarianisms of the counterculturists and New Leftists as "similar concepts." In fact, Rawls' notion of social justice is most often cited *apart* from the neo-Kantian philosophy that undergirds it, i.e., as a kind of free-floating egalitarianism.

For example, Rawls gives an uncharacteristically unadorned statement of his concept of social justice, which is one "that nullifies the accidents of natural endowment and contingencies of social circumstance as counters in the quest for political and economic advantage." This is often approvingly quoted or paraphrased by campus advocates of egalitarianism.

Rawls gives a more elaborate definition of his concept of social justice in section eleven of his book, albeit still unadorned by his Kantianism:

> I shall now state a provisional form of two principles of justice that I believe would be chosen in the original position...
>
> First: each person is to have an equal right to the most extensive basic liberty compatible with a similar liberty for others.
>
> Second: social and economic inequalities are to be arranged so that they are both (a) reasonably expected to be to everyone's advantage, and (b) attached to positions and offices open to all...
>
> All social values—liberty and opportunity, income and wealth, and the basis of self-respect—are to be distributed equally unless an unequal distribution of any, or all, of these values is to everyone's advantage.

Injustice, then, is simply inequalities that are not to the benefit of all.

Rawls builds his concept of social justice on a hypothetical social contract, after the fashion of Hobbes, Locke, Rousseau and others. But Rawls' theory of social justice is premised on what a highly "reasonable" person—in fact what *each and every* reasonable person—would choose in a "state of nature" *if* that state was conditioned so that it would preclude reason being distorted by irrational personal interests or biases. This is Rawls' reformulation of Immanuel Kant's "categorical imperative."

Rawls' condition for the "original position," his logical premise of a just society, is that each and every person would choose the idea of justice "behind a veil of ignorance":

> I shall assume that the parties do not know their conceptions of the good or their special psychological propensities. The principles of justice are chosen behind a veil of ignorance. This ensures that no one is advantaged or disadvantaged in the choice of principles by the outcome of natural chance or the contingency of social circumstances. Since all are similarly situated and no one is able to design principles to favor his particular condition, the principles of justice are the result of a fair agreement or bargain. For given the circumstances of the original position, the symmetry of everyone's relations to each other, this initial situation is fair between individuals as moral persons, that is as rational beings with their own ends and capable, I shall assume, of a sense of justice.

The last sentence in the quote refers to Rawls' explicitly stated premise, Kant's "categorical imperative," as formulated in Kant's *The Foundations of the Metaphysics of Morals.* "There is...only a single categorical imperative," Kant wrote, "and it is this: Act only on that maxim through which you can at the same time will that it should become a universal law." This imperative is *categorical* in that a moral action is done not for the sake of ends it may produce but for itself—as Kant put it, "not in the purpose to be attained by it, but in the maxim in accordance with which it is decided upon."

Kant's solely rationalistic moral philosophy, based entirely on "moral will" and without any concern with the *consequences* of actions, is moralism gone wild. An action that one knows in advance will have deleterious consequences is still to be done if the categorical imperative demands it; indeed one is obligated to do it. It is hardly a practical morality, and in fact it resembles a sort of fanaticism or madness.

Rawls' posited individual of pure reason stripped of any knowledge of himself in a state of nature is meant to present the purely rational man who can act on Kant's extreme principle of completely dissociated moral will. Yet, even as a hypothesis, what can Rawls' position mean? What can it mean to have "will" with no personal characteristics? It could only mean a disembodied, abstract, reason, without personality or character. But Rawls does speak of "individuals" and moral "persons," as he must, for only persons are capable of will. Even as a hypothesis, then, the notion fails, for purely rational moral will is not human in any recognizable form. A "social contract" between such—what shall we call them—"entities" bears little resemblance to human society, because it indeed bears little resemblance to the human condition.

The notion of a social contract has been employed as a useful hypothesis by many political philosophers, notably Hobbes, Locke and Rousseau. The concept is a logically constructed fiction that individuals existed before society. It does not pretend to be an anthropological hypothesis; if it were, it would be hard, if not impossible, to maintain. A presocietal, prepolitical, "state of nature" is posited. It is brought to an end by agreement of individuals to form a social contract or compact or covenant in order to create conditions for a better human life. Thus philosophers have found the fiction useful to speculate on what individuals would be like without society, and what obligations and rights individuals have toward society and vice versa.

But in order to speculate fruitfully on these questions, it is necessary that individuals forming the contract be recognizable as human. In the thinking of Hobbes and Locke, e.g., they are reasonable human beings, not entities stripped of all human characteristics except reason, as in Rawls' formulation. Devoid of all other properties and characteristics, such as body, personal experiences and interests, and emotional hopes, fears and attachments—and, in the case of Rousseau, man's natural moral character as a noble savage—why should such entities form a society? Where is the incentive? Such an entity of pure reason would be God-like, and such a God does not need others.

Rawls' theory, then, is essentially what its popularizers have made of it. It is absolutist egalitarianism, without regard to the consequences to individuals or society of a system "that nullifies the accidents of natural endowment and contingencies of social circumstances as counters in the quest for political and economic advantage." It is not the traditional, Lockean democratic ideal of equality of opportunity that seeks to even out the contingencies of social circumstances, but rather an egalitarianism that aims at equal results by nullifying accidents of natural endowment. For how can we know "accidents of natural endowment" except by their results, that is, individuals' excellent or-not-so-excellent performances? On American campuses since the mid-1960s, this egalitarianism has assaulted and sought to eliminate academic excellence as "elitist" by attacking all academic standards and distinctions that measure differences between students, would-be students, faculty members, would-be faculty members, and between competing curricula and courses.

Rawls' notion that inequalities should be admitted only if they "are to everyone's advantage" is not the important qualifier to absolute egalitarianism it purports to be. It puts the burden of proof on those who would maintain distinctions of quality, e.g., among the performances of people, and judgments about the quality of ideas, e.g., about curricula, courses and books. How can one prove that it is "to everyone's advantage" to judge that Shakespeare's dramas are better than TV soap operas, or that Mozart's music is better than Madonna's? It is no good to dismiss aesthetics from Rawl's consideration, for aesthetic judgments, it may be argued, are indeed factors "in the quest for political and economic advantage."

In addition, we may ask, how can one prove that it is to everyone's advantage to judge that astronomy is truer than astrology, or that a student who is bright and has studied should get a grade that is better than grades given to duller or lazy classmates? And what if it can be shown that it is to be in everyone's advantage to judge that soap operas are better than Shakespeare? It won't do to say that we would never come to that conclusion, for that is to admit that there are intrinsic differences in quality and that they hold regardless of "social justice"—the converse of Rawls' theory. Distinctions of quality are based in reality. But in principle, Rawls would have us justify them in the name of an abstract notion of social justice even if the notion should mandate that we judge astrology truer than astronomy if this is in the interest of social justice.

Distinctions of quality usually depend upon more "utilitarian" ideas of social justice than Rawls' absolute rationalism. Simply put, distinctions are based also upon the *consequences,* good or bad, of choices. Nowhere is this thrust more needed than in education, which is concerned with consequences—what kinds of people should colleges turn out, and for what purposes? In this sense, education is a supremely pragmatic enterprise. The pre-New Left rule that everyone is to be treated equally unless *relevant* differences between individuals have been demonstrated leads to concepts of justice that are less offensive than egalitarianism to sensible balances between the needs of individuals and those of society.

7.

Finances:
Facts, Fictions
and Fancies

IN OUR TIME, the practice of "looking to the bottom line" is vaunted as "tough minded." In fact, it has become perhaps the foremost shibboleth of a cynical period. In education, it abets still another dualism afflicting the enterprise, that of thinking of cost apart from meaning and quality. Of course, the palliative usually given, borrowed from politicians by those who perpetuate the dualism, is that by "good management," educational "excellence," or worse, "productivity," will be maintained or increased through "austerity" spending. It is first necessary to recognize that this is outright nonsense.

In a time of slogans, one of the better to come from the 1980s was, "If you think education is expensive, try ignorance." Charles Dickens put it more elegantly in *A Christmas Carol.* The Ghost of Christmas Present reveals to Scrooge the spectre of two wasted children, "wretched, abject, frightful, hideous, miserable in their humility."

Scrooge is appalled, and asks about the children, "Spirit, are they yours?"

"They are Man's," said the Spirit, looking down upon them. "And they cling to me, appealing from their fathers. This boy is Ignorance. This girl is Want. Beware them both, and all of their degree, but most of all beware this boy, for on his brow I see written which is Doom, unless the writing be erased."

Education is expensive, and growing more so. About $125 billion is spent annually on higher education in the U.S. *After* adjustments for inflation, tuition at private universities rose by 47 percent from 1980-81 to 1986-87, and by 35 percent at public universities. And while the inflation rate for the year ending July 1987 was 4 percent, the rise in tuition was 8 percent at private four-year colleges and 6 percent at public four-year colleges during the academic year 1987-88. This despite the fact that overall enrollment at colleges remained steady during the 1980s. By 1987, the average annual tab for tuition and fees at private colleges was $6,150, and the average at public colleges was $1,100.

One of the reasons education is costly is that it is inherently a "labor intensive" activity. The best education involves a low student-to-teacher ratio, in a seminar approach or a lecture mode of teaching. Today, despite high tuition, the low student-to-faculty ratio is in fact often honored in breaches. For example, according to *Time* magazine, some introductory classes at Harvard University enroll 1,000 students. And Harvard is hardly alone in this absurdity.

Low student-faculty ratios afford each student opportunity to ask questions of the instructor and to discuss the subject studied with the instructor and other students. Aids to this educative process, such as audio-visual material and computers, may supplement and enhance it, but to think they can replace ongoing student contact with an instructor is to believe in a *deus ex machina,* in this case *literally* creating a god from machinery to solve a problem. Unfortunately, financially pressed educational administrators, together with manufacturers of the machinery, form a powerful priesthood of the *deus ex machina* religion from whom we will continue to hear more as the costs of higher education continue to rise. Still, it is time also to say, in the very face of popular awe of electronic gadgetry, that this *deus ex machina* solution, too, is nonsense.

We would do well to keep in mind the conclusions of a hard-headed writer named Leon Wieseltier, who spent a night "talking" to an extraordinarily "smart" computer equipped with a very advanced program called "Racter," short for "Raconteur." Wieseltier found:

> Racter's charm began to wear off almost as quickly as it came on. Indeed, by morning I felt like the most dewy-eyed humanist...It is dead—deader than the deadest men and women who ever put pen to paper...There followed, that night, hours of exchange between the ghost in the machine and the *machine in the ghost.* [Emphasis added.]

But classroom labor intensity is not by any means the only reason or even the main reason for the high cost of high tuitions. In fact it is one of the least factors in the rise of college costs in the past three decades. Even beyond the very pertinent facts that faculty salaries *declined* some 20 percent in real earning power from 1970 to 1983, that 41 percent of all college classes are taught by part-time adjuncts paid subpoverty wages, and that in many courses the student-faculty ratio is absurdly high, the *non-instructional* expenditures of colleges account for the lion's share of their total costs. This is true in absolute terms, in terms of percentages, and in terms of increases in both absolute numbers and percentages.

A 1987 study by the Office of Educational Research and Improvement of the U.S. Department of Education (*Higher Education Administrative Costs: Continuing the Study*), documents that 20 cents of every dollar spent by colleges in the 1984-85 academic year was spent on administrative costs, an increase from 17.7 cents ten years earlier. The percentage of college employees who are faculty members during the same period of time *fell* from 32.2 percent to 30.8 percent, while the number of nonteaching "professionals" *rose* from 19.4 percent to 23.4 percent. (The remaining 46 percent of personnel consists of nonprofessional employees, e.g., secretaries, security people, grounds and buildings maintenance people, etc., a figure that *dropped* from 53.5 percent in 1966.)

To bring it to a point, the percentage of total costs colleges spend on actual instruction, that is, education, declined from 53 percent during the 1949-50 academic year to 49 percent in 1984-85. The money lost to education as such has not for the most part gone toward the advance of knowledge or the betterment of society. The percentage spent on research and public service hardly rose over a thirty-five-year period. Moreover in the years from 1976-77 to 1985-86 there was a decline in the percentage of overall expenditures for maintaining college libraries, and the same is true for expenditures for physical plant operations and maintenance.

Thus, many campus libraries have inadequate and ill-tended stores of books and periodicals. The cutbacks on maintenance also help explain the current crisis regarding campuses' physical plants, a crisis which when finally addressed will be enormously expensive. It is estimated that it will cost $30-40 billion dollars to renew higher education's physical plants. Fifty percent of buildings on American campuses date from before 1960, and 25 percent from before 1940. And the costs of equipment have climbed sharply, reflecting the equipments' ever-increasing sophistication. For example, the cost to equip an ordinary physics laboratory runs about $75,000, a sophisticated one millions of dollars, and one in high energy physics can cost over a billion dollars. In 1977, the University of Chicago annually spent $225,000 to equip its physiology and biology labs. Ten years later in 1987, the annual cost had risen to $1.4 million. Plainly, if the overall percentage of expenditures by colleges on equipment has not risen and the cost of equipment has risen at a high rate, then one must conclude that colleges are making do with old, scanty, obsolete and otherwise inadequate equipment.

In contrast, the increase in expenditures has occurred most sharply in administrative costs. Not including salaries of deans, this category includes "student services" contributing directly to students' academic, emotional and physical welfare, such as counselling, guidance and student health services. But mainly it consists of "institutional support," including "executive direction and planning" (i.e., the often inflated staffs maintained by college presidents, including non-academic "vice-presidents," "special assistants," "human resources managers," and other vague titles—the CEO model of the college presidency has taken on imperial dimensions), "legal and fiscal operations," "public relations," "fund raising," "general administrative services" and something the U.S. Department of Education calls "administrative computing."

Thus, from 1976 to 1986, while instructional costs (including library purchases) for all American colleges went up 21 percent, administrative costs went up 40 percent. At the University of California, for example, the number of administrators rose by 31 percent in four years, during which time the number of students rose by only 5 percent. Surveying the scene, Kenyon College Professor Thomas Short notes that "As administrators hire more administrators their power and sense of importance increase proportionately, as do the salaries they command."

For those believing in the creed of the greater efficiency of the private sector over the public sector, it is interesting to note first, that private college expenditures rose faster than public college expenditures; second, "private four-year colleges spent 35 percent of their budget on instruction and 30 percent on administration compared to 45 percent on instruction and 25 percent on administration at public four-year colleges;" and third, as put by Chancellor Joseph S. Murphy of the City University of New York, the distinction between "private" and "public" colleges today is "mostly a metaphor," at least in terms of financing. This last point refers to the fact that public funds (taxpayers) pay directly and indirectly for a significant share of the costs of private institutions.

The U.S. Department of Education study singles out the University of Georgia as typical of what has happened to higher education. For every 100 faculty employed at the University, seventy-two nonteaching "professionals" are employed; the number of nonteaching professionals has grown by 40 percent over ten years while the number of faculty has not changed. To use another trite phrase of our time, "It's good to see that colleges have got their priorities straight."

An understanding of why this is so takes us beyond money questions strictly speaking, despite bottom line enthusiasts, and back to the purposes of higher education.

One of the more important trends in higher education has been politicalization not only by campus radicals but also since World War II by *government,* resulting in cancerous legalism and bureaucratization on campuses. Much of the rising administrative costs of colleges is in fact to satisfy the red tape of federal and state bureaucracies, which, again like all bureaucracies, perpetuate and enlarge themselves by creating "needs" to address, i.e., more red tape.

A case in point is aid to students, which is so complicated and muddled that campuses employ specialists to cope with it—and many of the specialists privately admit they can't deal with it well. Worse, students are required to sort it out, beginning before they get to a college campus. Overburdened high school counsellors are usually not up to the task. According to the Executive Director of the National Association of Admissions Counsellors, the typical load of a high school counsellor is 400 students, and some have as many as 1,000 students. In addition, some 50 percent of those inquiring to colleges about applications are not high school students and thus have no access to counsellors at all.

In 1965, Congress passed the Guaranteed Student Loan (GSL) Program, the Educational Opportunity Grant Program (EOGP), and the College Work-Study Program (CWSP). In 1972, an additional Basic Educational Opportunity Grant Program (BEOGP) was created, since then named the "Pell Grants." In 1978, the Middle Income Assistance Act (MISAA) was passed. To be sure, money has gone to students—$4.8 billion through GSL by 1985, and $3.6 billion through the Pell Grants by the same year. Yet many students and would-be students have been daunted by the alphabet muddle of these and other programs and have not benefitted from them.

Writing in the February 1986 issue of *Atlantic*, Denis P. Doyle and Terry W. Hartle give an example of an actual "promising but needy" New York State student having to navigate the federal-state-campus-banks system:

> She was an "independent student" (her mother was dead, her father was unemployed, and she was on her own). In her senior year she faced tuition, fees, and living expenses of nearly $9,000. Her financial aid package included the following: a $1,700 Pell Grant, a $2,500 Guaranteed Student Loan, and a $500 National Direct Student Loan from the federal government: a $1,500 scholarship from her college: and $800 from her summer earnings.
>
> ...Of the federal government's major aid programs, three are administered on campus by college personnel, one is run by banks and state agencies, one by state governments and one by a private contractor.

Attempts at reform of the tangled system suffer the same types of obstacles faced whenever one attempts to change an entrenched multi-sided bureaucracy with vested interests in keeping the system tangled. The 13,000 banks which are making federally guaranteed profits from the GSL program join with campus specialists, whose careers depend on keeping the system mysterious, to advise Congress and state governments only to tinker with the system, preferably to make it more complicated.

Starting with the G.I. Bill of Rights period, American society at large, specifically through the federal government, committed itself to achieving equality in higher education. At first this meant equality of opportunity. But the unlikely alliance of the New Left and the federal bureaucracies in fact redefined "equality" to mean equality, or at least uniformity, of *results*. Colleges were fixed upon as both the means of achieving a more democratic society and the symbolic measure of how equal America is in fact.

As the process of collegial consensus disintegrated under the era's pressures on campuses in favor of "relevant" social issues, the government for its part stepped in and helped fill the vacuum with a mesh of rules, procedures, regulations, mandated guidelines, deadlines, protocols, and more other euphemisms for "control" than most people can summon from their vocabularies.

Previous to World War II, colleges were perceived, with substantial accuracy, as exclusive, discriminatory "clubby" institutions for the privileged elites, and, as used by the privileged, as all but "members only" training schools for their children to perpetuate their inherited superior status. To be sure, other goals of higher education from other periods of American history were still alive on campuses. Among these were the commitment to advance knowledge through research that was the legacy adopted from the German universities in the late nineteenth century, the agricultural/vocational emphases of the post-Civil War land grant colleges, the autonomy of liberal education, and even the religious/character training of colonial and early U.S. history. But to the public, and its elected officials, colleges were perceived as the "accrediting" institutions that gave the young who graduated from them entrance to the higher strata of American economic, cultural, and social life.

To a considerable extent, the last perception is still valid. It was estimated in the late 1980s that the life-time earnings of college graduates will exceed on average those of non-graduates by $640,000 each. And, understandably, an ever larger segment of the public since 1945 has wanted this income and other benefits of a college education. This is not to mention the perceived and eagerly sought larger advantages of economic and social opportunities enjoyed by those who are graduates of prestigious or "elite" schools.

In the period after World War II, the emphasis was on making America more like the democratic nation it had portrayed itself as being during the great war against facism. And in the 1960s, the civil rights and "anti-elitist," "anti-imperialist," anti-Vietnam War pressures accelerated and exaggerated the thirst for the ("participatory") "democratization" of America. The instrument chosen above all others to accomplish the goal was higher education. Two methods were used. Campus disruptions by counterculturists and New Leftists formed one jaw of the pincers applied to colleges. The other jaw was fashioned of the rebels' supposed enemy, the "establishment" mainstream political process, i.e., government. Government, and especially the federal government, entered into a new relationship with colleges, first as financial benefactor then, because a dispenser of largesse inevitably asserts its will, as rule-giver.

The results of what in recent years is increasingly being called the "partnership" of government and higher education are complicated and mixed. Tax levies are channelled into colleges on a scale not even dreamed of prior to the Second World War. And the opening of opportunity for millions of Americans in an expanded and in many ways enriched (at least before the late 1960s) network of higher education is one of the proudest accomplishments of post-World War II America. Despite all its ailments, the pluralism of American higher education is one of the reasons it has been admired throughout the world since World War II.

But all the great moral systems of the world caution that there are prices to be paid for "progress." The ancient Greeks expressed it in myths such as that of Prometheus, condemned to hideous torture for stealing fire from the gods on behalf of mankind. The Jewish-Christian story of the fall from Eden is rich in implications of the costs of human advancement. Chinese Taoists teach of the soul-distorting "imbalances" of the "masculine" aggressive forces of life over the "feminine" nurturing ones that usually accompany the assertion of even the most well-meaning social-political will. Hinduism's and Buddhism's sense of "karma" is much more than the concept of "fate" as Western popularizations usually render it. "Karma" is better explained as the sum total of all the moral consequences of all a person's actions over his entire lifetime, and by extension, of all of the moral consequences of the actions of a society or institution. It is the wisdom expressed in more homely fashion by an elderly Italian immigrant "shoe-shine boy" in response to a question of what he had learned from decades of living in the U.S. The man reflected for a moment, and said, "There's no free lunch."

It is the sum of the moral results of the evolution of today's politically supported, inspired, expanded, and altered mode of colleges that needs to be examined. If possible, the imbalances of the mode need to be corrected and a new balance established. The emphasis here should be on the word "new." If we take historical evolution seriously, we cannot just return to a previous time with its distinctive set of circumstances, any more than Adam and Eve could return to Eden. The analogy should not be taken literally. Pre-World War II, and pre-1960s higher education was hardly an Eden.

The trashing and trivialization of curricula, and the plunge from excellence are but some of the costs of what has happened. The bureacraticization and rule-mongering of higher education form other parts of its accumulated moral character resulting from its history of ever-expanding governmental-political intervention since 1945. Simply put, it means that, more and more externally dictated, inappropriate, confused or meaningless values, rules and regulations have been replacing and continue to replace achievement of authentic values and policies through a collegial process of deliberated experience by scholars and educators. In fact, since the 1960s, the imposition of a tangled mesh of expectations by society, and of legalistic values, rules and requirements by government on colleges has resulted in a crisis of the survival of higher education's soul. And that soul is *not* identical to the democratic American political process, however valuable that process is in expressing and achieving the political will of the people.

Questions of scholarly and educational judgments are not political, and education should not be servile to any goals external to education. Unless the American people and their government recognize and respect those truths, public-political financial support of higher education will continue to endanger the soul of the enterprise. This is indeed an American *tragedy,* in the true meaning of the word. The basically good American political character contains a basic flaw, which is potentially self-destructive by being poisonous to the free mode of higher education absolutely essential to American democracy. The American flaw is to exercise political will where it is not appropriate, and even more, where its exercise is destructive of the tender, fragile, and endangered essence of true education: academic autonomy and freedom.

The growth of the non-academic sides of college administration, then, is indicative of something much more critical than growing, burdensome tuition costs. (Still, it should be noted that the "no free lunch rule" is again evident here. Part of the moral result of the great effort to make colleges accessible to all has been a spiraling of costs that is making college education less accessible to the working class and poor.)

College administrations expanded to meet requirements of government red tape, and more ominous, their character has evolved not only to complement the governmental bureaucracy but also to mimic it. This has been still another reason for the dangerous splitting of administration from faculty in ways surpassing the traditional tensions between the two.

Traditionally, faculty were the source of academic values on campus and the administration the facilitator and enforcer of those values. But now administrations, in their increased public relations functions, take their values not only from popular trendiness and from pressure groups running the gamut from the political left to the corporate business world, but also and perhaps most, from politically partisan federal and state bureaucracies such as the U.S. Department of Education, the U.S. Department of Labor, the

117

U.S. Office of Civil Rights, and an almost countless array of other agencies. In the process, college administrations have become less and less an integral partner in the collegial educational process, and more and more a surrogate of government, business, and myriad pressure groups intrusively and dangerously disrupting and corrupting the collegial process.

Whatever the true or professed values of individuals who comprise them, college administrations are increasingly functioning as a fifth column, representing concepts of servile education in the midst of the camp of liberal education, to subvert liberal education. So, for example, colleges are moving away from the collegial model, which government, business and pressure groups don't understand or find an obstacle to their usurping colleges as *their* institutions. The colleges are moving toward a model that government, business and other groups find more familiar and much more manipulatable— the confrontational, adversarial "labor-management" model.

The adversarial model has questionable viability even in business corporations in today's post-industrial world, in which the U.S. is losing ground in economic competition. But it surely is a great mistake to reshape colleges in the form of this industrial model.

Yet it is happening. The faculty is seen, and many of the faculty understandably see themselves, as "labor." Again understandably given the imposition of the adversarial industrial model, about 30 percent of college faculty have unionized, a percentage far greater than the 18 percent of the American labor force as a whole. And administrators are seen and see themselves as "management."

Thus the sad spectacle of the U.S. Supreme Court accepting the model in a case known as *Yeshiva,* a decision as surreal in its specific finding as in its premise that colleges are and should be treated as examples of the industrial model. In the 1980 case involving Yeshiva University, the Supreme Court held in a 5 to 4 vote that faculty are "management" because they participate in the policy decisions made by colleges. To faculty who understand the double corruption of concepts involved in the Court's finding, their attitude toward it can be summed up in a quip attributed to Benjamin Franklin. When told the British regarded the American colonials as Englishmen despite Britain's curtailing of the traditional English rights of the colonials, Franklin is reputed to have answered, "Like the steer who has been called a bull, I am grateful for the honor, but I'd much prefer to have restored to me what is legitimately mine."

The health of higher education would benefit much more if college faculty were less "honored" as in *Yeshiva,* and instead have restored to them their legitimate collegial role as those responsible for the basic values of the enterprise of higher education. To complete the thought, the health of higher education would be better served if the collegial system were strengthened, and still another popular and more genteel fancy were dropped. This is the view that splits faculty from administration, and sees faculty as responsible for the "spirit" of higher education but not its "process," and administration as responsible for the process but not the spirit. This dualism of spirit and process is false in any human enterprise, and if continued will render colleges and universities asunder, mortally wounding higher education.

The critical problem then is not money per se, not the cost of higher education, but higher education's meaning, and therefore its *worth.* It is in this context that the financial problems of higher education need to be placed. Appreciating higher education's worth involves respecting that its supreme values are intrinsic to itself, that it should not be servile to other values, not even as an instrument of the most worthy moral or social reforms, and that liberal education is essential to the developed, free human spirit, which is in turn the *sine qua non* of a vital, modern democratic society.

Colleges, as they conform to government dicta regulating their "mere processes" in order to get government approval and funds, are in real danger of losing control of their essence and fate. The solution has to involve a wider public understanding of the invaluable, critical, and fragile nature of the collegial model and of liberal education, and a resulting public demand that government not impose its model on colleges in return for its financial support of higher education. This calls for a level of public intellectual maturity that is, unfortunately, hard to maintain at precisely that point where one's own political morality confronts the freedom of higher education. To put it plainly, people have to resist the temptation to yoke higher education to their most fervently sought moral, social, political, religious, or economic reforms. That will be possible only when enough people and their elected political representatives understand that a yoked liberal education is a contradiction in terms, and have the moral courage to respect academic freedom, authority, self-governance, judgement, and independence, by leaving the collegial process to reign autonomously over itself.

While the most rapidly and disproportionately rising share of the cost of higher education is administration, spurred on by government intervention, other components of the cost have been rising as well. Following experts on higher education finances, it is useful to divide these costs into two types. The first category of costs are termed "controllable," meaning, of course, that individual colleges have at least some substantial control over them. As examples, the individual college can decide how much to spend in any given year on books and periodicals for its library, and it can keep down raises in the salaries of its employees, including faculty. Uncontrollable costs are encountered where prices for goods and services required by a college are set strictly by the marketplace of the larger society. Examples include heating oil and other utilities' prices, the prices of laboratory and electronic equipment, and building construction prices.

Over many years before and into the 1980s, colleges held down their expenditures, and thus the tuitions they charged, by suppressing controllable costs, chiefly faculty salaries. To put it another way, the faculties of American higher education subsidized the education of millions of students by suffering incomes that dipped lower and lower under the rising cost of living, as measured, e.g., by the usual standard of the Consumer Price Index (CPI). In a study funded by the University of Hartford, Carol Frances demonstrated that when measured against the rises in the CPI, college faculty salaries in the U.S. declined 21 percent from 1974-1984. Another study showed that in real income terms, the typical tenured professor's salary in 1987 was 10 percent lower than in 1970, and faculty salaries were low in 1970.

During the decade from 1974-84, the costs of utilities tripled, the costs of books and periodicals rose by 150 percent, the costs of supplies and materials rose by 122 percent, the cost of equipment rose by 107 percent, the cost of *non-professional* salaries went up by 108 percent, the cost of contracted services grew by 101 percent, while the rise in faculty and other professional salaries rose by only 83 percent.

Moreover, the taxation policies of the federal government have been an additional uncontrollable factor in the rise of costs of higher education. As Carol Frances points out succinctly:

The employment taxes that colleges and universities pay *may exceed the total of employment plus income taxes paid by industrial firms* which are less labor intensive, and which have ways to shelter their income. [Emphasis added.]

The colleges and universities are exempt from income taxes but not employment taxes....Consequently, the label "tax-exempt" as applied to colleges and universities is becoming more and more of a misnomer, and ought to be dropped.

Who paid, then, and is paying now, for the increases in college costs? Aside from faculty, the most conspicuous group who stand out because of their individual burden consists of the payers of tuition. They paid 40 percent of the increases in college revenues from 1980 to 1984. But a more comprehensive look at who is paying for for higher education is revealing.

Total expenditures by higher education in 1984 were $86.5 billion. The federal government, which has imposed a constricting and costly "partnership" on colleges and universities, paid just $10.8 billion of this. Local governments paid $2.1 billion. As has always been the case, *state* governments (state taxpayers) paid most by far of the public support of higher education, and for that matter far more than any single private sector, contributing $24.6 billion. Of the *private* sources of income, tuition and fees accounted for $19.7 billion. Private gifts contributed $4.4 billion; endowments $1.8 billion; income from dormitories and bookstores $9.4 billion; other sales and services by colleges $1.9 billion; income from university-run hospitals $7 billion; and other sources $4.3 billion.

The other self-declared "partner" in higher education since the mid-1980s, corporate America, increased its contribution in 1984 to merely $1.5 billion, a record high. By any standards, then, big business is getting a bargain for the influence it is gaining on higher education, not to mention the myriad benefits in gets from higher education in the forms of an educated work force, and the results of research. Again, 50 percent of research done in the U.S. is by colleges and universities.

And it is colleges that are educating the largest growing sector of the work force, women. Female students, many of them from the largest growing group in the college student population, "nontraditional" older (over age twenty-five) students, made up 90 percent of the additional enrollment in public colleges from 1976 to 1983, and 74 percent in private colleges. In all, the number of nontraditional students jumped 79 percent between 1969 and 1984. Sixty percent of the nontraditional students are women, 70 percent of whom work full-time. It is estimated that by the mid 1990s, the nontraditionals will comprise a majority of all college students, and the large majority of these will be women, most of whom will also hold down jobs. Moreover the motivation of many nontraditional students accrues to business' benefit. Many go to school to get jobs or upgrade their jobs in the marketplace in the massive shift of America's economy toward the service and high technology sectors.

Who, then, should be paying for American higher education? When measured by benefits accrued and by ability to pay, corporate America comes first to mind as a sector which should be paying more. A "user's fee" tax on corporate profits to be spent exclusively for higher education is in order.

Increased public support of higher education inevitably raises hackles because of the fact that taxpayers are already paying a very high percentage of college costs, especially through state taxes (although the rate of taxation varies greatly from state to state—taxpayers of some states can plainly do more), and through federal taxes. Federal taxation raises the heated questions of priorities of federal spending, and the total amount of federal taxes Americans pay, considered burdensome by the middle class especially. These political factors are complicated by the enormous pressures and constraints of the staggering national debt, accumulated mostly in the Reagan years, which enabled Americans to buy, and become accustomed to, high expenditures on consumer goods and services. Getting Americans to give part of that "discretionary spending" power to taxes for higher education is a formidable political challenge.

Many people feel the "consumers" of college education, the students, should pay more of the share of the cost of their education. Thus there are calls and proposals for increased low-interest federally guaranteed loans to students. The loans would be repayable after the student is in the work force, and collected by the Internal Revenue Service as part of its income tax activities. This latter provision would solve the scandal of two million former students having defaulted on student loans, a default rate of some 10 percent, leaving taxpayers holding the bag. Some proposals call for indexing the rate of repayment to the total taxable annual income made by the former student.

By 1985, the Federal Guaranteed Student Loan program guaranteed $4.8 billion in loans by banks and colleges to almost five million students. Average debt incurred per borrower after four years of college stood at $9,000 for students at private schools and $6,700 for those at public schools. These debts by no means represent the terrible payback burden on young graduates depicted by the program's critics, especially since payback is over a long term.

Only about 80 colleges in the U.S. charge annual tuition in excess of $10,000. As a matter of fact, public colleges, which enroll a full 80 percent of all college students, as already noted, charge an average tuition and fees of $1,100. (Low tuition at the public colleges is a result of the already discussed fact that states pay the largest share by far of any single source contributing to higher education's income.) Americans' complaints about unaffordable tuition to a great extent really reflect their desire for expensive "elite" schools, and therefore the inordinate attention paid to their tuition levels. Yet another massive, but little-noted characteristic of the closing decade of the twentieth century is that in the rush toward egalitarianism. Americans want elite benefits for everyone, an exquisite self-contradiction. A case may be made that society at large is obligated to pay for each student's higher education; but how is it going to send all of its 12 million college students to Harvard?

Yet critics also point out that the increase of the federal loan program has been at the expense of a decline in *outright* grants given by the federal government to students, which are of course gifts entailing no obligation of payback on the part of the recipients. The proportion of federal aid to students given in the form of outright grants declined from 80 percent in 1975 to 48 percent in 1986. At issue here is the policy question of how much society at large is responsible for financing a student's college education, and how much responsibility should fall on the individual student. In the 1980s, the pendulum swung toward individual student responsibility, no surprise given the philosophical orientation of the Reagan and Bush administrations.

The Carnegie Foundation recommends an alternate scheme of federal student aid, at increased levels. It proposes that less student aid be given in the form of loans to be paid back in money, and more of it be in the form of grants to be "paid back" in the form of "service to society" after graduation, meaning of course unpaid labor or grossly underpaid labor. The idea is being advanced from all points on the political spectrum. For example, Democrats Gary Hart and Charles Robb each proposed a system of national service for all students, and William F. Buckley proposes that colleges require that prospective students spend a year in national service before admitting them as students.

The suggestion of service as pay for educational loans is seriously flawed.

If all young people are to be conscripted into government service, how is the money value of their labor going to reach colleges? Presumably, they would be doing strictly non-profit public service labor, and this does not create much taxable wealth. Alternately, assuming only those in need of college financial assistance would be put to labor, and assuming that their labor created wealth to be taxed, the idea smacks of indentured servitude—falling, of course, on the poorer classes, as indentured servitude always has. The rich would be exempt. The system would be like the scheme long advertised by the U.S. military—"join the Army and save your pay for college." Do rich young people do this? In addition, many of the present and future student borrowers are hardly young people. They are instead from the largest growing group of students, the older students. Again, it is estimated that in the 1990s a full 50 percent of the nation's college students will be older than twenty-five, and 20 percent will be over thirty-five. Many if not most of these students will have family and job obligations and commitments. For these reasons, they are hardly suitable for service in a "domestic Peace Corps." In fact, today some two-fifths of all college students work.

Moreover, the service-for-tuition proposal would yoke people to work they do not want to do, thus ensuring that the quality of the work will be dismal. Yes, in times of conscription the military does it—by martial discipline which denies the draftees many of their fundamental civil rights and liberties. The labor-for-college loans schemes no doubt would also involve barracks living and other aspects of semi-military or regimented life for many of the debtors. The rationale for military conscription is that it is necessary to the very survival of the nation. But do we want to impose military-style servitude on people simply because they are (or will be) in financial debt to the government? If the service is to be after college, as the Carnegie Foundation proposes, what of debtors who refuse to work or who do unsatisfactory work? Shall we put them in jail?

In addition, the programs proposed by the Carnegie Foundation and others are of grants—the federal government would *not* get its money back. These are no different than grants today except in their peculiar moralism that students do labor after receiving them, and only poorer students at that. Several colleges and states have come up with schemes of tuition loans of their own. For example, a proposal in Michigan would invite parents of newborn babies to invest $3,000 with a state agency, which would in turn use the state's privilege to invest the money *tax exempt* so that

124

enough would be there to cover four years at one of the state's colleges when the newborn eventually graduates from high school. If the high school graduate does not choose to attend a state college, the question remains of how to dispose of the money accumulated. To give it to the student to attend a private school, or not to attend any college, would allow, and invite, parents to exploit the tax-exempt investment status of the state for private purposes, a situation that is rich in corrupt possibilities.

Duquesne University has a similar plan, but for its alumni only. They can contribute $4,450 to the school to guarantee full four year tuition for each of their children eighteen years later. But the student *must* attend Duquesne, at least for two years, or forfeit the entire investment. Northwestern University uses its income-exempt tax status to float bonds to finance variable-rate low interest tuition loans.

The upper and middle classes in the U.S. show an enormous capacity to handle borrowing for everything from home mortgages to loans for cars, vacations, and virtually everything else imaginable. In fact, the motto of Americans since the double digit inflation of the late 1970s, if not before, seems to be "A penny saved is a penny wasted." It seems to be no violation of Americans' spending habits to suggest that students themselves directly pay for at least part of their higher education in a plan of low-interest loans, paid back over a long term with the rate of payback adjusted to actual after-taxes income, and collected by the I.R.S. as part of its income tax function. In fact, the I.R.S. has authorization from Congress to do something akin to this, and has been collecting on defaulted loans from some two million former students by withholding income tax refunds. The precedent is in place.

The 1980s closed with an unseemly irony. The academic world had been inappropriately politicized, while in the political sphere *proper,* that of public policies enacted by elected representatives, the larger society had temporized and failed to decide on how to pay for the expensive and increasing costs of higher education. That the decisions will have to be made is assumable, for it is inconceivable that in the 1990s America will prefer the prices of "choosing ignorance." It is inconceivable for many economic and other reasons. Most of all it is unthinkable because Jefferson's dictum holds stronger than ever: "If a nation expects to be ignorant and free, in a state of civilization, it expects what never was and never will be."

125

Index

academic affairs, 82-86
academic freedom, 42-43, 96, 99, 117
Adams, John, 30
adjunct faculty, 87
administrators, 10-11, 80-82, 90-91, 93, 111-14, 117-19
aid to students, 113-14, 122-25
Allegheny College, 32
American Association of Colleges, 71-73
American Association of State Colleges and Universities, 88
American Association of University Administrators, 82
American Council of Learned Societies, 102
American Council on Education, 65
A Nation at Risk, 4
A Nation Prepared, 91
Aristotle, 42, 53
Association of American Colleges, 65, 82, 90
Association of Governing Boards of Universities and Colleges, 80-81, 83
Association of Graduate Schools, 8
authority (*See* governance)
Avery College, 34

baby boom, 86-87

Basic Educational Opportunity Grant Program, 113
Beecher, Catherine, 33
Bennett, William J., 90
Berra, Yogi, 69
black colleges, 34
Bloom, Allan, 2, 44-56, 60
Boorstin, Daniel J., 2
Bowen, Howard R., 89
Boyer, Ernest L., 74
Boyer Report, 74-75
Brecht, Bertolt, 25
Brown, Rap, 48
Brown University, 31
Brown v. Topeka, 34
Brubacher, John S., 31
Buchwald, Art, 85
Buckley, William F., 123
Buddhism, 27
bureaucrats, 93, 113-14, 116-19
Business-Higher Education Forum, 4, 85-86

California Institute of Technology, 85
Cambridge University, 32, 35
capitalism, 61-62
careerism, 59-63, 66, 86
Carnegie Foundation, 27, 34, 88-89, 92, 123, 124
Carnegie Foundation for the Advancement of Teaching, 56, 67-69, 74

Carnegie-Mellon University, 101-2
Carter, Amy, 15
Catholic colleges, 33, 35
Central Intelligence Agency, 15
Chief Executive Officer, 80-82,
  86, 91-93
Chinese restaurant menu
  curriculum, 74
Chronicle of Higher Education,
  81, 92
citizenship training, 68-69
City College of New York,
  18-19, 21, 32
City University of New York, 16
civil disobedience, 15-16
civilization, Western, 39, 100-104
Civil Rights, Office of, 118
Clearing House on Higher
  Education, 84
coeducation, 34
College and University Personnel
  Association, 88
College of Virginia, 30
College Work-Study Program, 113
collegiality, 91, 118-19
Columbia University, 12, 19, 35
commercialization of higher
  education, 3-4, 43, 96
Commission on Strengthening
  Presidential Leadership, 80-81,
  92
competitiveness, 85, 93
computers, 110
Confucius, 64
content vs. process, 63-65
Cooperative Research Institute
  (UCLA), 26
core requirements, 73-77

Cornell University, 8, 19
corporations, 3-4, 59-60, 84-86,
  91, 93, 121-22
costs, administrative, 111-13,
  119-21
Council of Graduate Schools, 8
counterculture, 24-29, 58, 101-4
course load, 69-70
Cuomo, Mario M., 16
curriculum, 5-6, 29-37, 65-77

Dartmouth College, 93-94
Degler, Carl, 102
democracy, 17-18, 23-24, 39, 45,
  55, 74, 114-15
desegregation, 34
Dewey, John, 5, 64
Dickens, Charles, 109
dissertations, 8-9
distribution curriculum, 74
Doyle, Denis P., 114
Drake, George A., 82
drug culture, 17-18, 27-28
DuBois, W. E. B., 34
Duquesne University, 125

economy, the, 61-62, 68-69
Education, Department of, 111,
  117
Educational Opportunity Grant
  Program, 113
electives, 31-32, 65-66, 69-70
Eliot, Charles W., 32
elitism, 107, 115
Emerson, Ralph Waldo, 60
enrollment, 35-36
equality, 55, 104-8, 114-15
equipment, laboratory, 111-12

Evaluation Service (Michigan State University), 7

faculty, 10-11, 57-58, 71, 81-84, 86-91, 93-94, 110-11, 117-20
Faculty Participation in Decision Making (Floyd Report), 84
Fairleigh Dickinson University, 22
federal government, 113-19, 122-25
Federal Guaranteed Student Loan program, 122
feminism, 97
finances, college, 12, 109-25
Floyd, Carol E., 84
Floyd Report, 84
Flynn, Errol, 62
Frances, Carol, 120
free speech movement, 21
French Revolution, 22
Freud, Sigmund, 41, 47
fund raising, 81, 86

George Mason University, 88
Georgetown University, 35, 85
German universities, 18, 32, 35, 48, 51
Giamatti, Angelo Bartlett, 92
Golding, William, 24-25
governance, academic, 5-6, 17, 79-94, 82-84, 90-94
government regulations, 113-19, 122-25
grading, 7-8, 70
Graduate Record Exams, 8
Great Books, 50-51
Guaranteed Student Loan Program, 113

Guggenheim Museum, 25

Hart, Gary, 123
Hartle, Terry W., 114
Harvard University, 29, 31, 32, 110
Hegel, 44, 49, 54
Heidegger, Martin, 48
Higher Education Administrative Costs: Continuing the Study, 111
high school teaching, 90-91
Hirsch, E. D., 64
historical process, 50, 54
Hobbes, Thomas, 105, 106
Hoffer, Eric, 57
Hoffman, Abbie, 17, 48
Hook, Sidney, 103
Hooker, Michael, 66
humanities (*See* liberal arts)
human nature, 53-54

income sources, college, 121-22
indoctrination, 97
in loco parentis authority, 5, 92
intelligence, free, 39, 41-43
Internal Revenue Service, 122, 125

Jackson, Jesse, 101
James Joyce Memorial Theater, 25-26
Japan, 68
Jefferson, Thomas, 30, 31, 125
Jesuits, 33
Jews, 35
Johns Hopkins University, 12, 35
justice, 95, 104-8

Kant, Immanuel, 105-6
Kelly, Eamon M., 82
Kennedy, Donald, 100-101
Keohane, Nannerl, 34
Kerr, Clark, 80
Kerr Commission, 80-81, 92
King, Martin Luther, Jr., 16

Labor, Department of, 117
labor-management model, 118-19
League for Innovation in
  Community Colleges, 87
lecture method, 33
liberal arts, 31, 57-58, 88
liberal education, 50-51,
  59-77, 95
libraries, college, 111
Lincoln, Abraham, 31
Lincoln University, 34
Liquid Theater, 25-26
loans, student, 122-25
Locke, John, 105, 106

majors, 72
Marcuse, Herbert, 52, 100
Marx, Karl, 54
Marxism, 48-49, 97-99
Massachusetts Institute of
  Technology, 32, 88
McLaughlin, David, 93-94
Melville, Herman, 60
Mencken, H. L., 3
Mexico, 49
Michigan, 124
Michigan State University, 7
Middlebury College, 59
Middle Income Assistance
  Act, 113

Middle States Association of
  Colleges and Schools, 86
Morehouse College, 34
Morrill Act, 31-32
Murphy, Joseph S., 87, 112

National Association of
  Admissions Counsellors, 113
National Center of Educational
  Statistics, 8
National Coalition of Universities
  in the Public Interest, 4
National Endowment for the
  Humanities, 5, 67, 89-90
National Institute of Education,
  69-71
National Research Council, 8
natural law, 45, 51-54
Naziism, 48
New Left, 15, 17, 20-24, 29,
  43, 44, 48-52, 59-60, 84,
  96-108
Newman, Frank, 68
Newman Report, 56, 68-69, 72
Nietzsche, 29, 47, 48
1950s education, 63
1960s education (See Vietnam
  era)
Nisbet, Robert, 2
Noble, David F., 4
Northwestern University, 125

Oberlin College, 34
Office of Technology
  Assessment, 66
Ollman, Bertell, 100
open society, 43, 52, 95
Oxford University, 32, 35

paideia, 39
participatory democracy, 23-24
part-time students, 70, 121
Pell Grants, 113
personnel and budget
    committee, 11
PhD programs, 8-9, 35
physical plants, 111-12
Plato, 43-45, 54, 103
pluralism, 39
politicization of higher education,
    44, 47-48, 99, 113-19
politics, campus, 10-11, 91
Popper, Karl, 43, 54
prelection (teaching method), 33
president, college, 11, 80-82,
    85-86, 91-94
Princeton University, 35
private colleges, 112-13, 123
*Prospects for Faculty in the Arts
    and Sciences: Demand and
    Supply*, 58
public colleges, 31-32, 112-13,
    123

Queens College (CUNY), 16, 19,
    86

Radcliffe College, 85
rationalism, 45, 51-54
Ravitch, Diane, 2
Rawls, John, 3, 104-7
Reagan administration, 122-23
recitation, 32-33
reform, educational, 40-43, 85-86,
    89-91, 94
Reich, Robert, 64
relativism, 51

relevance, 57
Rensselaer Polytechnical
    Institute, 32
required courses, 65-77, 100-104
research, 2-4, 35, 89-90
revolution, 22, 49, 97-100
Rice, Stuart A., 9
Robb, Charles, 123
Robespierre, 22-23
rock music, 45-46
Rousseau, 23-24, 48, 49, 105,
    106
Rubin, Jerry, 48
Rudy, Willis, 31

salaries, 4, 87-88, 111, 120
Savio, Mario, 21, 48, 58
Schuster, Jack H., 89
seminar approach, 33
senate, university, 79-80
service-to-society proposals,
    123-25
servile education, 96
sexual activity, 47, 54
Shakespeare, 102
Short, Thomas, 112
Smith, Adam, 61
social contract, 105-7
social science, 54
Socrates, 16
Speaking for the Humanities, 102
Speigel, Melvin, 93
Spock, Benjamin, 48
Stanford University, 100-104
star system, 88
Stewart, Donald M., 82-83
student-faculty ratio, 110
students, 12, 70, 79-80

sunshine laws, 81
supermarket curriculum, 74
supply-and-demand, faculty, 57-58
Swan, Patricia, 79
Sykes, Charles J., 3

taxation, 120-21, 122
Taylor, Harold, 6
teaching, 3, 89-90, 110-11
tenure, 3, 86-87
thinking, critical, 95
Third World, 49, 97-99
Tolstoy, 28
To Reclaim a Legacy (NEH
  report), 67
*Trustee Responsibility for
  Academic Affairs*, 83
trustees, 82-86
tuition, 2, 4, 110-11, 121, 123

United States, 39, 97-100
universities, 35
University Centers for Rational
  Alternatives, 19
University of California, 112
University of California at
  Berkeley, 21
University of California at
  Irvine, 88
University of Chicago, 9, 85, 112
University of Georgia, 113
University of Hartford, 120
University of Massachusetts, 15

University of Minnesota, 79-80
University of Notre Dame, 85
University of Tennessee at
  Knoxville, 88
University of Virginia, 31

Vassar College, 34
Vietnam era, 5, 7, 11, 15, 17,
  20, 22, 25, 49, 50, 59, 65,
  104
Virginia Plan, 31
vocational education, 7, 31,
  57-63, 66, 86

Waller, Gary, 102
Washington University, 12, 85
Wellesley College, 34
Weltanschauung, 41
West, the, 49, 100-104
West Point, 32
Wieseltier, Leon, 110
Wilberforce College, 34
Wolfe, Alan, 96
Women's College Coalition, 34
women's colleges, 33-34
women students, 121-22
Woodstock, 27-28

Yale Report of 1827, 31
Yale University, 29
Yeshiva case, 118-19
yuppies, 27, 58

FREEDOM HOUSE BOOKS

General Editor: James Finn

YEARBOOKS

Freedom in the World: Political Rights and Civil Liberties,
annuals from 1978-1990

STUDIES IN FREEDOM

Escape to Freedom: The Story of the International Rescue Committee,
Aaron Levenstein; 1983
Forty Years: A Third World Soldier at the UN,
Carlos P. Romulo (with Beth Day Romulo); 1986. *(Romulo: A Third
World Soldier at the UN,* paperback edition, 1987)
Today's American: How Free?
edited by James Finn & Leonard R. Sussman, 1986
Will of the People: Original Democracies in Non-Western Societies,
Raul S. Manglapus; 1987

PERSPECTIVES ON FREEDOM

Three Years at the East-West Divide,
Max M. Kampelman; (Introductions by Ronald Reagan and Jimmy
Carter; edited by Leonard R. Sussman); 1983
*The Democratic Mask: The Consolidation
of the Sandinista Revolution,*
Douglas W. Payne; 1985
The Heresy of Words in Cuba: Freedom of Expression & Information,
Carlos Ripoll; 1985
Human Rights & the New Realism: Strategic Thinking in a New Age,
Michael Novak; 1986
To License A Journalist?,
Inter-American Court of Human Rights; 1986.
The Catholic Church in China,
L. Ladany; 1987
Glasnost: How Open? Soviet & Eastern European Dissidents; 1987
Yugoslavia: The Failure of "Democratic" Communism; 1987
The Prague Spring: A Mixed Legacy
edited by Jiri Pehe, 1988
Romania: A Case of "Dynastic" Communism; 1989

FOCUS ON ISSUES

Big Story: How the American Press and Television Reported and Interpreted the Crisis of Tet-1968 in Vietnam and Washington,
Peter Braestrup; Two volumes 1977;
One volume paperback abridged 1978, 1983

Afghanistan: The Great Game Revisited,
edited by Rossane Klass; 1988

Nicaragua's Continuing Struggle: In Search of Democracy,
Arturo J. Cruz; 1988

La Prensa: The Republic of Paper,
Jaime Chamorro Cardenal; 1988

The World Council of Churches & Politics, 1975-1986,
J.A. Emerson Vermaat; 1989

South Africa: Diary of Troubled Times
Nomavenda Mathiane; 1989

The Unknown War: The Miskito Nation,
Nicaragua, and the United States,
Bernard Nietschmann; 1989

Power, the Press and the Technology of Freedom
The Coming Age of ISDN
Leonard R. Sussman; 1989

Ethiopia: The Politics of Famine; 1989

Racing With Catastrophe:
Rescuing America's Higher Education
Richard Gambino; 1990

AN OCCASIONAL PAPER

General Editor: R. Bruce McColm

Glasnost and Social & Economic Rights
Valery Chalidze, Richard Schifter; 1988